On the Shores of Darkness

THE MEMOIR OF ESTHER KEMENY

ESTHER KEMENY

THE HALLER COMPANY

BURLINGAME

Copyright © 2003 by Esther Kemeny. All rights reserved. Printed in the United States of America. No part of this book may be used or reproduced in any manner whatsoever without written permission from the publisher except in the case of brief quotations embodied in critical articles and reviews. For information, address The Haller Company, 337 Beach Road, Burlingame, CA 94010-2005.

ISBN 0-9743961-7-6
Library of Congress Control Number: 2003112358

Book design: Heather Haller
Photographs provided by the author.

For Sam and Susan

CONTENTS

Preface		ix
Chapter 1	Michalovce	13
Chapter 2	Bratislava	47
Chapter 3	Return to Michalovce	55
Chapter 4	Meeting George	63
Chapter 5	Life with George	69
Chapter 6	Sered	87
Chapter 7	Liberation	97
Chapter 8	Finding George	111
Chapter 9	Post-War Life	115
Chapter 10	New York City	125
Chapter 11	Wellsville	133
Chapter 12	Chicago	139
Epilogue		142
Acknowledgements		143

There is properly no history, only biography.
Ralph Waldo Emerson

PREFACE

I am no writer, no artist, no deep thinker. Aside from a few attempts in my adolescence, I have never written. Lack of leisure, so necessary for literary growth, and lack of confidence in my talent were but two of my reasons for not persevering: In my native country of Czechoslovakia, the words of an artist are greatly valued. My teachers there had discouraged me because they thought that Jews could not be good writers. Then later, when my life turned hard and dangerous, there was neither opportunity nor inclination.

Decades have passed and now I choose to write. My reasons are clear. I would like this book to be a testament and memorial for future generations and for my two grandchildren to know what their grandparents survived and transcended.

Esther Kemeny, San Francisco, June 2003

"Esterl, my beloved come back to me!

Can you know how beautiful it will be when you return? We shall take walks into the woods. Under our feet, there will be a carpet of moss and fir needles. In the air, the birds will sing, and the pines will surround us with their fragrance. We shall hold hands and run a little.

Only us, the two of us alone—no one else will see us. What a joy it will be. And we will come to a lake, with a boat waiting for us.

From the sky—or heaven?—the sunshine will pour down on us in a flood. And I will sit down close to you, my dear soul, in the boat.

We will keep silent, looking quietly in the distance. You will be dressed in bright colors. Flowers of the field will be in your hair. And all around us the silence will be glorious. Only the angels from heaven will smile down on us and over the waves and the breeze to play for us the melody of unending love.

And we shall remain long, very long above all, only ourselves, from the shores listening to mysterious and beautiful sounds…"

George Kemeny, 1945

CHAPTER ONE

Michalovce

My life began in 1912, in a country marked by political upheaval. I was born in Michalovce, a small town along the Laborec River in eastern Slovakia.

In 1912, Michalovce was a quiet town, anonymous to world history. No one outside the region knew much about the town or its people and no one expected great deeds from either. The only cues to a world larger than itself were the river and the rail that cut through the center of the town. The rail took the seasonal harvests from the Zemplín region's fertile lowlands and the beer from our town's largest factory. It was the way we traveled to the nearby bigger cities of Kosice and Presov, and to Bratislava, one of the larger cities in western Slovakia.

I was the first child born in our home on Main Street, in a four-unit building that my family had built the year before my birth. We lived in one of the two apartments in the rear of the building. On the Main Street side of the building were two stores. The one in front of our apartment was leased to the owner of a school-supply store. The other one was leased with the apartment behind it—first, to a hatmaker, then to the owner of a shoe store.

Main Street was in the center of Michalovce's busy downtown. On one side of our home was an inn, on the other a synagogue. City Hall stood just across the street. Nearby, there were markets, several schools, a café, a hotel, a cinema, a Hasidic synagogue, and Greek Orthodox and Roman Catholic churches. About a mile from our home at the edge of downtown, where Main Street turned to dust and darkness, stood the train station.

Michalovce was my mother's town. She was born there and most of her family lived there—in fact, many of them right on Main Street. Her brother Simon ran the inn next door to us, the same inn that her father once owned. A few doors down was her sister Salli's grocery store, which was just steps away from her brother Ludwig's. Her sister Regina, who married well, lived on the other side of us, several doors down, along with her husband, daughter, and three sons. Regina's husband owned an electrical plant and a flour mill—the same mill where her brother Armin worked when he was not running an inn near the train station.

Although Uncle Ludwig's grocery store was closer to our home, my mother usually sent me to Aunt Salli's store to buy things, because Aunt Salli and Uncle Moritz had ten children and were very poor. Their struggle was obvious: My uncle could not afford to keep their store well stocked, so if I was sent there to buy a pound of sugar, he had to go to his wholesaler to buy it before he had any to sell to me.

Uncle Moritz was a very good man. He was intelligent and very religious. On weekdays, he sat near the counter of his long narrow store with his hat on his head and a blanket on his lap and pored over his Talmud. All of his children were self-educated and all six of his sons became professionals: two were lawyers, two were doctors, and two were accountants.

When the Gottlieb boys were attending university in Bratislava, they were able to support themselves by teaching and by relying on food donations. The oldest son was an accountant who lived in Budapest. He married his first cousin and had one daughter. The second oldest was a rabbi who later became a medical doctor. One day, after he married a rich girl and received a large dowry, I asked him, "Why do you let your father sit in his cold store all day long, where there is no heat? Why don't you help him out?" He replied, "Esther, I do support my father. I know that he cannot make a living from the store; but, were I to take it from him, he would certainly die of depression. He needs people in his life, coming into his store and talking with him."

My father was born about ten miles from my mother in the tiny village of Zavadka. He was the first of ten children born to Leopold Berkowitz and Elke Moskowitz. Leopold was an innkeeper by trade. The family lived next door to their inn on a thirty-acre farm—a place I would return to every summer.

My father left Zavadka for the United States at age sixteen, a year before he would be required to serve in the national army. He went to Scranton, Pennsylvania, by then a booming industrial town with an established Slovak population. While living in America, he worked as a store clerk and studied English and jujitsu in his spare time. In 1892 he became a U.S. citizen and three years later—eager to marry and settle down—he returned to Slovakia to find a mate. He met my mother, Josephine Brügler, in Michalovce, shortly thereafter, and in 1900, their first child, Ilona (Ilonka) was born.

The seven of us—my parents, my sister Ilonka, my older brothers Ignatz (Icu), Aaron (Ari), Alex (Sanyi), and I, the youngest—lived in our little apartment on Main Street, along with a poor peasant girl named Marca who helped with our daily chores.

While we were not one of the poorest families in town—that title reserved for the Gypsies living amongst us—we lived under rustic conditions.

Because our town had no running water, we relied on a nearby well for our water and wood-burning stoves for our heat. Our toilets were three outhouses in the backyard that were daunting to use in winter: Snow fell between the wooden slats of the structure and froze the seats inside and often they were teeming with large frenetic rats.

With no bathroom or plumbing at our disposal, we bathed in our day room, a small room near our kitchen. A good deal of our time was spent in this room. It was not only where we bathed, but where we ate all of our daily meals, studied, and where my three brothers slept. Crowded into this small room were a table with seven chairs, a bed with a trundle bed stored under it, and a small wood-burning stove. Every night like clockwork, a tiny visitor spied upon my brother Sanyi in the day room as he studied his law books. We called him the Midnight Mouse.

My sister and I slept in a single bed in an alcove next to the day room. The alcove was just large enough to fit a nightstand and lamp next to our bed. Our mattress was a straw-filled sack covered by a large sheet and a thin feather-filled cover. We had several big feather pillows and slept under a linen-covered feather bed, called a *dunyha* in Hungarian, and a *perina*, in Slovak.

Our apartment was always ice cold in winter. I

was afraid of the dark, so every night before going to bed, I put a glass of water on my nightstand, to avoid a trip into a dark kitchen in the middle of the night. In water, that water had turned to ice by the next morning.

To help warm our beds at bedtime, my mother rubbed a hot brick across our bottom sheet or tucked a hot water bottle under the covers. Sometimes the cork fell out of the water bottle and the water spilled out onto our bed. Several years later, my parents built a ceramic-tiled stove in their bedroom and the heat from two logs burning in it kept everyone in the house warm through the night.

A curtain hanging in the doorway separated my parents' bedroom from the alcove. In their bedroom were two single beds, two night tables, a wardrobe, a dressing table, and a tall chest of drawers for storing linens. At the foot of their beds was a chaise longue—my father's favorite place to take his afternoon nap.

The centerpiece of their dressing table was its three-paneled mirror. Flanking the large center mirror were two smaller mirrors attached to the center one by hinges. As a child, this mirror charmed me. I used to lie on my father's chaise longue to view myself from the front and adjust the smaller mirrors to see what I looked like from the back.

A pair of French doors separated my parents'

bedroom from our formal dining room, a room that was reserved for holidays and guests. Across the hall from our dining room was a pantry. It was a large room lined with shelves and had windows that faced the plum and pear trees growing in our yard. I remember once, when my mother locked me in the pantry as punishment for misbehaving, I took it as an opportunity to eat some of the delicious fruit that was stored in one of the jars on the shelves.

Our kitchen was large and kosher. In it, there was a wood-burning stove, a credenza for storing dishes, and two tables—one for dairy and one for meat. A gallon of fresh milk from my uncle's farm was delivered to our home every morning. Sometimes, my mother skimmed the buttermilk off the top of milk and churned it into butter. Each morning after attending morning prayer service my father went to the kosher butcher shop down the street to buy our daily meat. When he came home, he removed the meat from the wrapper and placed it on the meat-only table. Then he rubbed salt all over it and soaked it in water according to kosher custom. As he prepared the meat, my mother prepared the day's vegetables.

My father enjoyed cooking and was very good at it, but rarely did so because it was considered "woman's work." If someone came to our door while he was helping my mother cook a meal, he would nervously flee the kitchen. I felt sorry for him that it made him so uncomfortable.

Animals always served a function in our household. We had a dog that caught rats and a cat that caught mice and a small pen of chickens and geese in our backyard that we kept for food.

During World War I, the Austro-Hungarian Empire put my father into a position of buying and selling horses for the army. His job required him to ride the train. To make his way home from work at night, he had to walk along a darkened street leading from the train station to our home. Because he knew jujitsu, he was not afraid of anything—during the daylight. But one night, when he was carrying an especially large amount of money from a day of selling horses, as he sat on the train he started to dread his long walk home. The money he was carrying was not his own and he feared someone might try to take it from him. When he stepped off the train in Michalovce, there at his feet was our dog, Pityu, ready to greet him. My father was never so thankful to see Pityu because he thought that a dog could hear an approaching stranger and give warning.

Behind our house, we grew a small garden of garlic, onions, kohlrabi, parsnips, carrots, and cabbage.

In the fall, we canned some of the fruit from our trees and much of what grew in our garden. We did not own a refrigerator or icebox. To keep fruit fresh for awhile, we wrapped it in newspaper and stored it on top of one of our wardrobes. To keep root vegetables fresh for a few days, we buried them in a large sandbox that we set behind the ladder leading to the attic, just off the kitchen near Marca's private room.

As children, we looked forward to the farmers markets every Friday—especially during the summer and fall. That's when a wagon filled with watermelons traveled our streets in the early evening. The watermelon vendor always gave us children big juicy slices of watermelon to taste. Fall was also the season for making sauerkraut. Making sauerkraut was very exciting because it was such a large-scale event. My family would purchase a wagonload of cabbages from the farmers market and rent a large cabbage shredder for the day. Then Marca would lay a large sheet on the floor and begin the daylong chore of shredding all of the cabbages. We would add some kosher salt, onions, and occasionally small apples to the pile, then everything on the sheet was poured into a large wooden barrel. A wooden disc, slightly smaller than the diameter of the barrel, was placed directly on the cabbage and topped with large, heavy stone disc. After a week or two of fermenting, the sauerkraut was ready to eat.

In the winter, our geese moved into the attic. We gave them plenty of water to drink but no food. Instead, Marca kept them abnormally fat and nearly immobile by force-feeding them greased corn twice a day. This rich meal made them balloon to twenty or more pounds and fattened their livers to two or three pounds. After three or four weeks of this torturous feeding ritual, the geese were slaughtered, plucked, and hung in our pantry by their feet. Since our house was always cold in the winter, the goose meat stayed naturally fresh in our pantry. Marca and her friends pulled the goose feathers off of their stems and put them away to use as extra down feathers. We cooked the goose heart and used the bones, gizzard, and wings for soup. We filled the gooseneck with stuffing and made pâté from the liver. From the breast meat, we made gooseburgers that we breaded and fried like a cutlet. We added bread to the meat to extend it into a few more meals. We relied on the geese for all of our fat because we could not feed our chickens well enough for them to produce much fat.

One twenty-pound goose fed the eight of us for three or four days. In the winter, we ate goose every Friday. On cold winter Fridays, we especially liked to eat *griven*. Griven is made by frying chunks of fatty goose skin with a little bit of goose meat. After the fat turns to liquid, the mixture is forced through a sieve. The crispy fried skin that remains in the sieve is *griven*.

Marca made bread for the family twice a week. In the evening, she put some flour, boiled potatoes, yeast, leaven, and a little water into two large containers and let the dough stand overnight. The following morning she kneaded the dough, wrapped it in a clean towel, and placed it in a basket. After the dough rose, she took it to the local bakery, where it was baked into two glistening, wheel-sized loaves.

In the winter, our noontime meal was often soup—usually beef-and-potato or a delicious soup made from goose, carrots, parsnips, celery, onions, garlic, and noodles. Our evening meal, or supper, was a light one. In the winter, it might be large white radishes or pickles; in the summer, a glass of buttermilk with some of Marca's delicious homemade bread topped with butter, lettuce, green peppers, or radishes.

On Sabbath, when my mother could not get real fish, she made "mock gefilte fish" from chicken breast. On Sabbath, we also ate cold fish stew or soup.

In those days, washing clothes was a grueling household chore. One day a month, Marca rose at one in the morning and worked until midnight just doing the laundry. She began by fetching water from the well behind the synagogue next door, hauling two buckets of water at a time to the kitchen. After she heated the water over a kitchen fire, she scrubbed the clothes by hand, using a washboard and soap that my mother made from animal fat. To produce a bleaching effect, she added ashes to the hot water. When she was finished washing the clothes, Marca and several of her friends hauled the clothes to the river to rinse them out. During the winter months when the river was frozen over, she would wrap the freshly washed clothes in a sheet and, axe in hand, carry the heavy parcel on her back down to the river in her bare feet. When she reached the river, she cut a hole through the ice and began to dip each piece of laundry into the river below. This practice made my mother very nervous. Not only did she worry about Marca's feet, she feared that one day a piece of our laundry might slip through her hands and be lost into the depths of the river. But my mother never expressed her concerns to Marca because she knew how much Marca looked forward to spending time with her friends at the river. When Marca came back home from the river, she hung the clothes on a clothesline in our attic.

As a young girl, I thought my family was rich because we had a home, enough food to eat, and a maid. I saw others in town who had less.

Gypsies lived in abject poverty in shanties at the edges of our town. None of my friends nor I had any idea why they seemed to be so helpless. Nobody seemed to feel any pity and compassion for their position and no one was willing to help them. Non-gypsies believed that Gypsies stole what other people left out. People who stole did so because they were poor. Peasants stole butter and eggs because they were hungry and could not get enough to eat. Most of the peasants in the villages around Michalovce were small farmers who worked very hard for little reward. It was a struggle for them to feed their large families, so many of them sent their teenaged girls into the towns to live and work as maids. These girls were paid a dollar a month salary and felt fortunate to be able to work in the towns. Their new position offered them what they could not get at home: enough to eat, a room of their own, and a small amount of spending money. Because of the living arrangements, most of a maid's basic needs were provided for. In two or three months, a peasant girl working as a maid could earn and save enough money to buy herself a skirt.

While my parents could not afford to buy me pretty dresses, once a year I did get a new dress and a new pair of shoes for Passover. Often my new shoes would wear out before the next Passover, so to help keep the snow off my feet, I would stuff newspaper inside of them.

I did not want to be different from those who were less fortunate than I, so I always wore my new dress a few days before Passover. On Passover, when my friends would ask me, "Esther, is that a new dress?" I was able to say, "No, it is an old one."

My siblings and I rose at six in the morning every day and started our day with a bath. To begin to prepare for our baths, Marca checked the buckets of water stored in the kitchen to make sure there was enough water in the house. If we needed more, she brought some in from the well, then lit a fire in the kitchen stove and heated the water on the stove. To warm the day room for our baths, she gathered some of the leftover cinders from the kitchen fire and put them in the stove in the day room. Then she brought pitchers of fresh and hot water into the room and poured a little water from each into a large bowl set on a chair that we used as our wash basin.

To conserve fuel, we left the heat in the kitchen stove on all day, but put out the day room stove when we left for school. It was lit again when we came home at noon for dinner and remained on through the rest of the day until it was time for bed. On cold winter days, my mother spent her afternoons in the day room, where she read and did her handiwork.

My mother was a plump, sweet-natured woman, full of joy and laughter. She enjoyed singing around the house and was quick to delight in everyday things. One of her favorite sayings was, "I am fat because I laugh so much." She was very easygoing, warm, and loving to us children.

As young girls, my cousin Jolanka and I used to accompany my mother to the public bath every month when she went there to bathe in the *mikvah*. The *mikvah* is a specially designed pool of water that, according to the Jewish custom, purifies whomever or whatever is immersed in it. As part of this kosher ritual, my mother had to be washed clean in a separate tub before she was allowed to enter the *mikvah*. While she was being scrubbed clean in a large sunken bath, Jolanka and I sat on the tub's two inner steps and washed in its warm shallow water. Imagine, four people sharing the same bathtub!

When I was older, I would go to the public bath at least once a week and before special occasions. The public bath offered a variety of personal services: I could get a massage; a facial; and have my hair washed, set, and styled. When I returned home, all that was left for me to do to prepare for an evening out was to put on my best dress.

While our family were observant Jews, I did not have a religious lifestyle. My father thought that girls did not need to learn about religion, so I did not read the Bible or go to the synagogue very often. My personal religious rituals were limited to fasting at Yom Kippur and praying twice a day for those who were sick.

My father rose every day at five in the morning to study the Talmud. Every day he attended morning and evening prayer service at our synagogue next door, which was the most magnificent and imposing building on Main Street. Synagogue members were required to buy lifetime seats. Since we were poor, my family sat in the less-expensive seats in the back of the synagogue. My wealthier aunts and uncles sat up front.

On holidays, my father brought home soldiers from the synagogue to celebrate the festivities with our family. On those occasions, we lit some candles and made wine spritzers by adding a little seltzer water to the wine. After the white cloth was placed over the challah, my father said a prayer over the bread and tore off a piece for everyone at the table. Then he said the blessing of the wine and offered us all a small glass of wine.

My father was a loving man, but a strict disciplinarian. Whenever my brothers did something bad, he would take off his belt and spank them with it. This form of punishment distressed my mother making her plead to him, "Don't spank them so!"

When Sanyi was about fourteen years old, he felt the brunt of my father's disappointment. He had stopped studying, so my father said to him, "If you do not want to study, you will have to learn a trade." Then he took off his belt and spanked him with it. After that, Sanyi studied very hard and finished first in his class at graduation.

"They can take away your money. They can take away your trade. But you will always have your education," were words my father said to us often.

No doubt my father learned the value of education from his father, whose literacy afforded him success and prominence in his community. My grandfather was the only man in Zavadka who could read or write, and as such, was a heavily relied upon member of his community. Villagers often stopped by his inn to ask for help with their legal papers and correspondence.

Because my father was one of the few people in Michalovce who had learned English, he later found himself in a similar situation. The weekly farmers markets always drew a large crowd of townsfolk and peasants into downtown Michalovce. When the topic of immigration to America came up at the farmers market, invariably, my father's name would be mentioned. Immigration hopefuls often stopped by our home after their trip to the market. My father would offer them a glass of slivovitz and wrote letters to immigration officials for them in English.

In Michalovce, the Jewish community appeared to be better off than others in town because, on the whole, the Jews were better educated. While Jews had always believed in advancement through learning, anti-Semitism, which was already prevalent in our schools, only increased the pressure for Jews to succeed. But I knew of some Jews in town who were very poor.

Mrs. Sandman, a Jewish widow from Poland, lived behind us in a small house with tiny windows and doors and an earthen floor. She lived there with six of her seven children. Her seventh, whom I never met, was living in America. Mrs. Sandman was a dwarf. Two of her children, one son and one daughter, were also dwarves.

Because their home was so tiny, Mrs. Sandman's two boys slept in their small kitchen and Mrs. Sandman and her four daughters slept in another, slightly bigger room. I do not know how Mrs. Sandman was able to support all of her children, but

I believe it was most likely through her skills as a naturopath. She knew all about herbs and their medicinal properties. In the summer, she picked blueberries and made jars of preserves from them. She always took a jar to those who were suffering from diarrhea. As part of her natural pharmacopoeia, she applied herbs to infected sores, used leeches to draw out the blood of hypertensives, and performed cupping to treat those with pneumonia. Cupping is an ancient folk remedy in which small glass cups, which we called "bunkies," are heated then turned upside down onto a person's back. The suction between the hot glass and the skin increases circulation to the area, which some believe stimulates the immune system.

Mrs. Sandman once told me that my headaches were caused by the "evil eye." To confirm her suspicion, she dropped a few cinders into a glass of water. When the cinders sank to the bottom of the glass, it indicated to Mrs. Sandman that her diagnosis was correct. To cure me, she dipped her fingers into the water and then stroked my forehead with her hand.

Mrs. Sandman also earned money by making *lungenwurst* for the townsfolk. *Lungenwurst* is a type of sausage that is traditionally served at Jewish weddings. Making it is a long and laborious process. Mrs.

Sandman would scrupulously wash the full length of cow intestines inside and out. Then she stuffed segments of it with a mixture of cooked ground cow lungs, peppers, onions, and rice. When a six-inch length of intestine was filled, she tied it off and stuffed another, until the all of the intestines were filled.

I thought Mrs. Sandman made the best piroshki—big ones filled with potatoes. My family ate tiny piroshki filled with cheese and raisins or topped with jelly, but Mrs. Sandman's were quite different from those and very delicious. Because she knew how much I enjoyed her piroshki, whenever she made them, she invited me over for dinner. My mother was unhappy if I accepted. She would ask me, "Aren't you ashamed to eat up what the poor woman has?" I would reply, "Give her my potatoes, soup, and meat and in exchange I will eat her piroshki."

When Mrs. Sandman's children were older they supported themselves. Her dwarfish son became a shoemaker and her other son became a horse trader. Two of her daughters, including the dwarf, became housekeepers. Another daughter, named Hanca, became a seamstress.

Hanca was my best friend and playmate. We had a wonderful time playing together. We chattered away as children do and enjoyed playing make believe.

We did not own any real toys, nor did we have a real doll. Instead, my mother fashioned one for us. She tied two twigs together in the shape of a cross to make the doll's arms and legs and stuffed two rags to make a head and a body. She made a face for the doll by adding three dots of black ink to the head.

Hanca and I loved this little doll. We played with it for hours on end. Sitting in the grass near her house, we sewed doll clothes and pillows for it from little scraps of material and made doll hair from corn silk. The doll traveled around the yard in a little buggy made from a shoebox that we pulled along by a thin piece of string. Often my cousin Jolanka joined us in our games. She was the same age as I and lived right next door. The three of us liked to jump rope in the front of our house and play hopscotch and jacks made from little stones.

On Saturdays, we liked to play house. Each of us would bring over a little goody to eat, such as a small piece of cake, candy, or fruit. On occasion, uniformed soldiers from the nearby army barracks would march down our streets accompanied by a military band. We loved to watch this parade. One Saturday, as my friends and I were playing house, Sanyi and his playmates came in to tell us that the soldiers were approaching our street. Eager to see the procession, my friends and I dashed outside. While we were out watching the procession, Sanyi and his cohorts stayed inside and ate up all of our food.

Sanyi, who was two years older than I, relished his role as my tormentor. The two of us fought all of the time and he spanked me many times. Because I was the youngest child, I was pampered and spoiled. This may have contributed to our sibling rivalry. All Sanyi had to do to provoke me was look at me sarcastically and I would burst into tears. When my mother would ask me why I was crying, I would sniffle, "Because Sanyi is looking at me." She would snap: "Because he is looking at you? He has eyes; what should he do?" Her response did not sit well with me.

Sanyi's favorite pastime was going to the cinema. Back then, our movies were silent films with captions. When I was too young to read the movie captions, Sanyi struck a deal with me. He offered to tell me the movie's story when he returned home if I would give him all of the pocket money that I had saved up. I gladly accepted his offer because I did not like to be alone in my bedroom at night and always welcomed a bedtime story. When he returned home around seven or eight in the evening, he came into the alcove and sat beside my bed. I looked at him and said, "Tell me the story now, Sanyi." He sat silently for a moment, then said, "Give me a moment to think." While I waited for him to gather his thoughts, I fell asleep. The following night, I asked him again to tell me the story and he replied, "I have forgotten it." I fell for this trick many times.

Although he exasperated me as a child, when we were older, we became very good friends. He started to watch over me like a mother hen, just like my sister and other two brothers.

It was a long journey from my home in Michalovce to my grandparents' farm in Zavadka; yet, every year I was sent there for two weeks in summer because my mother thought that I needed to breathe the "good air" on the farm. I traveled to the farm by myself. The trip began with a train ride to Humenné, where a horse-and-buggy coach waited to take me the rest of the way.

On the farm there were a half dozen horses, cows, chickens, geese, and a large garden filled with fruits and vegetables. Two or three farm hands were there to help my grandparents maintain it. When I summered there, only one unmarried aunt, Teresa, was still living at home. Because my grandparents' living quarters were small, I had to sleep in the same bed as my Aunt Teresa. I did not like my aunt. She would take me down to the freezing cold river to bathe me and push my head under the water to rinse my hair before I had learned how to hold my breath underwater. It felt as if I was drowning.

Most of my days on the farm were spent at my grandmother's side. My grandmother was a very kind and loving woman. She cooked well and baked all of the time and was the farm's resident beekeeper. I marveled at how she managed to scrape the honey off the honeycombs without ever being stung.

To dry out her large, freshly washed urns she hung them like ornaments on the branches of a big tree. There, they swayed all afternoon under the sun. I enjoyed much of the time I spent on the farm with my grandmother, except when she forced me to drink fresh cow's milk straight from the cow, still warm and foamy and not yet sterilized.

In 1919, when I was six years old, my carefree childhood passed away in an instant. Before 1919, Michalovce was part of the Austro-Hungarian Empire and was known by the Hungarian name, *Nagymihaly*. But by mid 1919, the Versailles Treaty had dissolved the Austro-Hungarian Empire and Czechoslovakia had become a self-governing nation. This new republic was plagued by post-war instability. Within a few short months after Czechoslovakia had declared its independence, a communist revolution began to stir in the area. It was led by Aaron Cohen, alias Bela Kun, a Hungarian journalist of Jewish ancestry.

Before the outbreak of World War I, Kun was accused of embezzling a large amount of funds from the Hungarian Workman's Cooperative Society and fell into disgrace. Then, in 1916, as a soldier in the Austro-Hungarian army fighting on Russian soil, he was captured by the Russians and imprisoned. Kun was a born socialist and a lightning rod for the Revolution's new communist ideology. While in prison, he began proselytizing other Hungarian prisoners of war. Lenin eventually appointed him a Minister of Propaganda, and at armistice, Kun returned to Hungary to win it over to Bolshevism. Furnished with a false passport and disguised as a Red Cross doctor, he and a group of fellow revolutionaries crossed the border into Hungary.

Before Kun had left Russia, Lenin had given him money to start a communist newspaper in Hungary. The paper promised to improve social conditions in the country and to rid the country of Romanian forces, through Russian help.

Kun's propaganda proved highly effective. In the spring of 1919, Hungary's acting president Count Károlyi resigned and surrendered his government to a communist coalition headed by Kun. Shortly thereafter, Kun sent troops into Slovakia to reclaim it for Hungary.

This action led to fighting in our part of the world.

One day the Hungarians were in our town, the next day, the Czechs. At night, my family spent more time under our beds than in them. As the conflict escalated, my father went to his hometown of Zavadka to see if there was fighting there too. There was none.

While he was away, the sound of the cannon blasts grew louder and my mother became increasingly frightened for our safety. One night, around two or three in the morning, she told us it was time to flee. Ilonka, who was nineteen years old at the time, Ari, who was eleven, and I—along with my mother, Aunt Hermina, and cousin Jolanka—left home on foot. This was just after harvest and the fields were very dry and prickly. Because Sanyi did not have any shoes on—I assume he could not find them—he could not walk with the rest of us as we headed for the fields surrounding Michalovce. I do not know where he went, but I believe Jolanka's brother, Willie went with him.

After traveling a brief distance, my mother had to stop. She was obese and suffered from arthritis in her knees, so she was unable to walk long distances. We decided that Ilonka, Ari, and my mother would hide in a cornfield and that Aunt Hermina, Jolanka, and I would walk to the nearest village. While we were making our way to the next village, drunken Czech soldiers discovered my family hiding in the cornfield. The soldiers told them that they were going to be taken away and shot. But a Czech officer intervened and assured my mother that they would not be killed because they were only looking for Bela Kun's men.

When Aunt Hermina, Jolanka, and I arrived at a nearby village, we stayed with an old Jewish woman whom my aunt paid to feed and house us. We soon discovered that the fighting was as heavy in the village as in Michalovce. Again, we were hiding under our beds every night.

For the few days that we stayed there, the Jewish woman offered us potatoes and buttermilk to eat. Jolanka and I ate outside sitting on little stools beside a *hokerli* table, a miniature side table that was ill-suited for dining. On one occasion, as I was mashing a full plate of potatoes into the buttermilk, I accidentally dropped the entire plate of food into the mud. I thought that our hostess would be very upset with me and that I had lost my one meal for the day. Because her cupboards were nearly bare, I was surprised when she offered me a second helping. Now, every time I eat a baked potato with sour cream, I think of this kind old Jewish woman.

When the fighting ended, Hungarian soldiers drove us in their truck back to my aunt's home. Aunt Hermina's parents were living with her and had stayed at home during the fighting. When we arrived there, everything looked the same as before we left.

Then I walked next door to my house. There, I found the windows and doors broken, the house plundered, and no one at home. I was seven years old and felt all alone. I knocked on a neighbor's door. When she answered, I asked her if she knew where my mother was. She said, "No, I don't, but maybe the Hospodars will know." The Hospodars were friends of my mother who lived nearby. I ran through the garden that separates our home from the Hospodars', hopeful that they would know where my mother was. Again, I was met with disappointment. I began to cry as I walked down the alleyway towards the gate that separated the alleyway from the street. Then, as I neared the gate, I saw my father heading towards me. He comforted me and said, "I will buy a horse and buggy and we will go look for our family."

As we approached the train station in our new horse and buggy, I spotted my seventeen-year-old brother, Icu, armed with a rifle and guarding the train station. I was baffled by the sight because there was no more fighting in the area. I do not know which army gave him the gun; the only thing I remember is the gun on his shoulder. My father asked Icu if he knew where our mother was. Icu told us that she was staying at my paternal Aunt Regina's home in Trebisov, a town about ten miles from Michalovce.

Aunt Regina's house was very small—just two

rooms plus a hall and a kitchen—and on that day, very crowded. My aunt, her husband, and their children were staying in one room. My mother, Ilonka, Ari, and my two maternal aunts, Salli and Regina, and their children were in the other.

When we were certain that the fighting was over, we returned to our home in Michalovce and began to rebuild our lives.

Within a few months, Kun's dictatorial regime was ousted and the official language of my school changed from Hungarian to Slovak. At the time, I already spoke Hungarian, German, and a regional dialect of Slovak that is closer to Polish than Slovak. I spoke Hungarian with my parents and my siblings; German with my grandparents; and the Zemplín dialect of Slovak with Marca and most of the townsfolk. My parents also spoke Yiddish to each other. Though my father knew English, I rarely heard him speak the language. The only English he taught us children was the lullaby, "Rock-a-bye-Baby."

At age twenty, Icu went to study in Vienna at Hochschüle Für Welthandel, a graduate school in International Trade. My parents paid his tuition and his room and board. At the same time, Ari was attending business school in Michalovce and Sanyi was in Gymnasium. Ilonka was a dentist in Trencin, a town in western Slovakia.

That same year, after four years of elementary school, at ten years old I entered Gymnasium, a highly selective eight-year secondary school in Michalovce. To be accepted to Gymnasium, I had to pass a difficult entrance exam. Because of its high standards, graduates of Gymnasium were accepted to any university in Europe.

Strict rules were in effect at Gymnasium. Students were not allowed to date or wear cosmetics during the eight years they were enrolled. Permission from a professor was required to see a movie and a year-round curfew was in effect. Students had to be in their homes by seven in the winter and eight in the summer. If a student broke any rule or received failing marks twice, he or she was expelled from the school. Classes began at eight in the morning and ended at four, with a one-hour dinner break at noon, when the students went home to eat with their families. Every night there was three or four hours' worth of homework to do.

All of the courses at Gymnasium were obligatory and the curriculum was rigorous and unrelenting. We studied algebra, geometry, chemistry, astronomy, physics, geography, and history, in addition to several languages. In the first grade, I took Slovak, German, and Latin; in the third grade, French was added.

I was good in math, but not able to excel in Slovak because my professors discouraged the Jewish students. They told us it was not in the national interest for Jews to learn how to write and speak well. Likewise, my history teacher insisted that I study Czechoslovak history from a different book than the others in my class. He told me that I needed to learn more than the others because "Jews must know three times more than non-Jews to pass this class."

Out of the one hundred fifty students who were enrolled in my class, twenty-one of us graduated. There were only six girls in my class, three of whom were Jewish. I graduated first in my class.

In 1927, my father became ill from pemphigus vulgaris—a rare, often-fatal autoimmune disease that affects the skin. Blisters formed all over his body and in his eyes, nasal passages, and esophagus. He was in constant pain; his skin felt as if it were on fire. Doctors admitted him to the Prague German Clinic, a teaching hospital, where they kept him in a bath of lukewarm water to prevent anything from touching his skin.

One early morning as he lay in his bed, he felt that he was about to die. He rose out of his bed, pulled a sheet onto himself, and said the prayer for the dead. Then he lay back down and fell asleep. As he slept, he heard a voice say to him, "You will not die" and a few minutes later he felt a tingling all over his body.

When the professor of dermatology came in to see him the next morning, he said, "Mr. Berkowitz, what did you do?" My father asked him why and he replied, "You are cured!" It was a miracle.

After my father's spontaneous remission, he was released from the hospital with strict orders not to smoke, drink, or work, because his doctors thought that avoiding physical and mental stress might help prevent a relapse of his condition Now it was up to my brothers to provide for our family.

Over the next few years, painful blisters continued to form under my father's arms and in his groin. To ease his pain, I injected morphine into him every day. Because I was afraid he would become addicted to the morphine, when his blisters started to clear, I slowly tapered off his dose by diluting it with distilled water. One day, I injected him with pure water and he did not know the difference. He said, "Esther, I think we should start reducing the dose, now" and I replied, "Daddy, I already have. This is only water."

That made him uneasy, but he never asked for morphine again.

Postcard of downtown Michalovce in 1910.

Esther's parents in back of their home on *Main Street in Michalovce.*

CHAPTER TWO

Bratislava

In 1931, after graduation from Gymnasium, I was enrolled in law school at the University of Bratislava. Bratislava is about two hundred twenty four miles from Michalovce or a twelve-hour train ride from home.

The government-backed university did not charge tuition to good students, but still there was room and board to pay. Sanyi had enrolled in law school the previous year and my family could not afford to pay room and board for the both of us.

Originally, I wanted to go into medicine, but in medical school, the professors took roll call. This meant that I would be required to attend all of the classes. Since I could not afford to live in Bratislava for the four-and-one-half years of enrollment, I chose to become a lawyer instead. I stayed at home in Michalovce and got a part-time job doing clerical work. Sanyi loaned me his first-year law books to study from and I studied law at home eight hours a day.

I lived near the university only when I needed to be there during the examination periods. When I first came to Bratislava, I roomed with a schoolmate. We ate cheaply through a Jewish organization that offered us discounted food and occasionally my mother sent me care packages. Once, after a relative told her how much she had saved by sending a package to her son as a sample at the lowest postal rate, my mother sent me some goose liver the same way. To secure the liver for the long journey, she surrounded it with three hard little apples. When the package arrived, all that was left inside the parcel were the apples.

In Bratislava, I studied intensively for about twelve hours each day. I did not attend any of the lectures. To help me learn the material, I met with other law students at the local coffeehouse and together we studied and tested one another.

At the end of the third semester, or a year-and-a-half of study, I took my first round of examinations. The first round of tests to be taken in each subject were called comprehensive examinations. As with most of the tests at the university, the comprehensives were oral examinations. Comprehensives were held in a large auditorium and open to the public. During the sessions, professors sat at a long table in the front of the auditorium and students were called up to the table and tested on the subject by the professor who taught the course. Anyone could attend the testing sessions and listen in as a student was being tested.

Students often sat in on the sessions to help them learn the material. Once you passed the comprehensive test, to pass a course you had to take a second test, a final examination called the *Rigorosum*. The *Rigorosum* was an intensive, in-depth examination held privately in the professor's office in which the professor questioned you on the subject for one or two hours. The second series of examinations were held in the eighth semester, when there were two more rounds of comprehensive and *Rigorosum* examinations.

After I passed my first round of comprehensives, I returned to Michalovce and began to work part time in the law office of my cousin, Joseph Brügler. For three dollars a month, I took dictation and wrote letters to lawyers affiliated with the cases that we were handling.

During my summer breaks from school, Ilonka and I often vacationed together. Not far from where she lived was a well-known spa in Trencianske Teplice. We often traveled there to visit the spa and to enjoy the live music and dancing on the outdoor terraces of the nearby hotels. At the time, Ilonka was a young widow. She had married a dentist when she was in her late twenties, but after a year of marriage, her husband died suddenly of a heart attack. At age forty, she would marry her second husband, Zoli Farkas, a dental technician who worked in the same dental practice as she.

In my eighth semester of law school, I returned to Bratislava and studied twelve to fourteen hours a day. My brother Ari, who by that time was the vice president of a bank, noticed that I had been losing a lot of weight from not getting enough to eat, so he arranged for me to live with a family in Bratislava. My room and board was twice as much as before, but Ari paid it for me.

When it came time to take my criminal law comprehensive test, my criminal law professor said to me, "You know the law very well, but I have never seen you at the lectures." There were only ten female students in my class, so it was not easy for one of us to go unnoticed. I said nothing back to him, for he was right. I never attended his lectures. Because of my absence from class, the professors held a conference to determine whether I should be allowed to pass the exam because I knew the subject so well, or should be required to take one more semester of school. The professors wanted me to take another semester, but the dean disagreed, so I was allowed to pass the comprehensive exam. I did well on the *Rigorosum* test and passed it too. In April of the following year, I took my third and final round of comprehensive and *Rigorosum* examinations and passed them, entitling me to receive my doctorate of law.

In May of 1936, when I was twenty-three years old, I became the first woman from Michalovce to graduate from law school.

My father traveled to Bratislava to see me receive my diploma. He arrived on a Friday, the day before the graduation ceremony. I put him up for the night in a nearby hotel. When I went to pick him up the next morning, I found him eating breakfast in the hotel's coffee shop without his hat on. Startled by what I saw, I said the obvious: "Father, you do not have a hat on." He replied, "My child, you do not see anyone else with a hat on. I cannot stick out like a sore thumb." Then he paid for his breakfast. Observant Jews usually wear hats in public and do not handle money on the Sabbath.

"Father, it's Saturday!" I gasped. He replied, "Yes, I know, but the Talmud says that even on a Saturday you should pay for a service right away, so the one you owe does not think you are trying to cheat him."

My father occasionally could surprise me. As a teenager, I used to love to swim and play volleyball. When I was eighteen years old, I wanted to buy a swimsuit that had shoulder straps that crisscrossed in the back. I thought my father would disapprove of the style, so I took it home to try it on. My father was lying on his chaise longue about to take a nap. When I went into his room to show him the suit, he looked at me in the swimsuit and said, "Very nice. At least your back will get a suntan." I asked, "Can I buy it?" and he said, "Sure." I was certain he would say no, that it revealed too much of my back.

Esther in Trencin.

CHAPTER THREE

Return to Michalovce

After law school, I returned to Michalovce to live at home while I looked for work. At the time, Icu and Ari were vice presidents of banks. Ari, who was not yet married, was living at home, helping to support my parents and me.

In 1936, it was hard for a woman to find work in the law field. I wanted to be a judge, which, at the time, was a nearly impossible achievement because Jews were seldom awarded judgeships. Right after graduation, a friend who was a newspaper vendor put an announcement in the Hungarian newspaper in Kosice stating that "Esztika" Berkowitz of Michalovce received her doctorate of law. When I read the notice, I became indignant. I felt emancipated and proud of my achievement and thought that the use of the diminutive form of Esther—a term of endearment usually applied to little girls—was denigrating. I asked my friend, "What is this? Did a first grader receive her doctorate?"

On Sundays in Michalovce, the dance hall offered a five o'clock tea. For a penny, I was served tea and cookies, and listened and danced to live music. One Sunday, after I had just returned home from law school, I decided to go to the dance hall. That afternoon, Ari came home and asked my mother, "Where is Esther?" My mother looked around and said, "I don't know. She was just here." She went into her bedroom, opened the wardrobe, and noticed that my dressiest dress was missing. Both of them assumed I went to the movies, so Ari went there to join me. At intermission, after he realized I was not in the theater, he walked over to the dance hall. When he spotted me there, he came up to me and asked, "Esther, may I have this dance?" then proceeded to dance me right out of the hall. I was twenty-three-years-old and a doctor of law, but still he scolded, "Now you will be grounded for a week. You will not be permitted to go to a movie. You will not get a penny!"

This was not unusual behavior for my brothers. All three of them carefully watched over me, monitoring my activities and making sure that my needs were met. For years, when my parents could not afford to buy me any dresses, Ilonka and my brothers bought them for me.

When I was just starting out as a lawyer, there was New Year's Eve ball that I wanted to attend. At the time, I only had a long wool dress to wear. Ari gave me money to have a more suitable dress made for the ball. I designed the dress—a long black satin gown that had a skirt with side slits, a stand-up collar, and a long silver rope belt bearing my initials. The dress made me look somewhat like a monk, but I was pleased by how I looked in it. After the dance, to make better use of the dress, I cut it in half and made two blouses from it.

In 1937, I worked briefly in the law practice of Dr. Fleischacker in Bratislava. Later that year, I moved to Humenné to work in the law office of Dr. Grün. Humenné was a small town about eight miles north of Michalovce. Criminal cases were not tried in Humenné but in the larger city of Kosice, about thirty-five miles away. If our firm took on a criminal case, we paid lawyers in Kosice to represent the case for us and administered the cases through written correspondence. We wrote in Hungarian, Slovak, and German, depending on where the crime took place. This was most efficient way for us to handle these kinds of cases because most of us did not own cars and the trains did not run frequently enough to make daily round-trip travel possible.

While in Humenné, I lived in a small room in a widow's home. One night, a group of boys at a local coffee shop came to my home and began to serenade me. I was embarrassed by their display. When they had finished, as tradition dictates, I signaled my acceptance by turning the lights on and off three times. When I saw that the boys had awakened my neighbor, I became even more embarrassed as I told my neighbor that I was sorry for disturbing her. She replied, "Don't be. It was beautiful and I enjoyed it."

During my law school years, stories about Hitler and the Nazis began to appear in our newspapers. Hitler was flouting the Versailles Treaty by vowing to unite all of the Germans into one state. Because of its large German population, Hitler took immediate aim at Czechoslovakia. In 1938, he overran the Sudetenland, the German part of Bohemia.

That same year, I began working full-time for my cousin Joseph in his law firm in Michalovce, where I earned seven dollars a month. Joseph did not have much money, but he was a very kind and charitable man. Every Friday he added an extra dime or penny to my salary for me to give to the *yeshiva bochers* from Silk Street.

Silk Street was a district in Michalovce where the Hasidic Jews lived. The Hasidim were easy to distinguish because their men wore side-curls and did not trim their beards. They were strict adherents of Judaism and the Torah and did not send their children to Gymnasium or associate with us Orthodox Jews.

In contrast to our grand synagogue on Main Street, the Hasidic synagogue was set inside a small and unassuming house. Many of the sons of the Hasidim were *bochers*, or students of the Talmudic academy. I do not know how the Hasidim made their living. I only know that each week the *bochers* came into our neighborhood and received money from my cousin Joseph and others.

While I was working in my cousin's law practice, Sanyi worked at the law office of Max Brügler, our mother's cousin. Because I had a doctorate of law, I was able to hear cases in court. Joseph and I once took on a small claims case in which one peasant stole a bundle of hay from another. Sanyi's firm was representing the opposing side, so it was Brügler against Brügler and Berkowitz against Berkowitz. Because Sanyi was a very smart man and a very good lawyer, when the case was about to go to court, my father said to me, "Don't let Sanyi beat you! Fight for yourself!" In the end, the judge threw out the case, leaving the plaintiff and defendant to pay their lawyers, so no one really won.

I did not enjoy practicing law. Some lawyers were cruel and merciless. Crooked lawyers took advantage of many poor, illiterate peasants. When a peasant got a notice from the court reminding him to appear in court or to pay a settlement, he would not know what to do with it. A series of notices would follow stating that all of his belongings were going to be auctioned off if he did not respond. Without even knowing what was happening to him, a peasant could lose all of his property.

Once I was involved in a case where we had to take away a poor man's only cow. This incident marked a turning point for me. I was hurt by all of the injustices I witnessed and began to despise the law. I thought that if I could become a judge I could change these things.

Ari, Esther, and Sanyi.

CHAPTER FOUR

Meeting George

While there had always been a strong undercurrent of anti-Semitism in Czechoslovakia, in 1939, it surged. Following the resignation of its president, Edward Benes, the Czechoslovak republic fell apart. By March of 1939, Slovak fascists ruled Slovakia, led by Father Josef Tiso, a Catholic priest who was elected Slovakia's president. Although Tiso expressed opposition to the "Nazification of Slovakia" and tried to distance himself from fascist ideology, pro-Nazi radicals dominated his government. Six months after the fascist takeover of Slovakia, Bohemia and Moravia were transformed into a German-controlled Protectorate.

That same year I was disbarred. I was no longer allowed to practice law because I was a Jew.

In 1939, I also met my future husband, George Kemeny, strolling along a popular promenade in Michalovce called the *Corso*. The *Corso* was a wide, brightly lit sidewalk on Main Street, where people walked arm-in-arm with their friends and greeted passersby. In summer, the air along the *Corso* was sweetened by the fragrance of roses and lilacs that bloomed along the walkway. One day in late summer, as I was strolling the *Corso* with three of my male friends, I met Lily, a young physician whom I knew from school. With her was another young doctor named George Kemeny.

"Who is that good-looking girl" George asked Lily, glancing back in my direction as we passed each other. She replied, "Dr. Esther Berkowitz." Then George asked her, "Is she taken?" When Lily said that she did not know, George asked Lily to introduce him to me. Lily replied, "How can I introduce you to her? She is with three other young men." Never one to shy away from something that he wanted, George told her to think of an excuse to talk to me. So Lily came up to me and said that she had regards from my sister, who lived in the same town as Lily's fiancé. Then introduced me to George. After we exchanged a few pleasantries, my friends and I continued on our stroll.

Despite our fleeting encounter, I could not help thinking about the man I had just met. His sweet demeanor, his black hair, and his soft skin tickled my heart in a strange and interesting way. While I had many male friends in college, there was something about George that seemed different. This man, I said to myself, would make a good husband. This man, I would love.

I had heard of George from a friend who was a pharmacist in town. He said that George was one of the best students in his class and that he had a remarkable reputation. In fact, George was a brilliant man with an extraordinarily high IQ. He was one of the best medical students that the University of Bratislava had seen in twenty years. Until his last exam in medical school, George had a perfect academic record. But, if George were to earn the highest grade on his very last exam, the university would be compelled to honor his achievement with a public ceremony. Just before his final exam, one of George's professors had forewarned him: "George, do not study for your last exam because it will not be worth it. The school will not give you the highest grade because you are a Jew."

The day after I met George, I went to the Strand, a popular riverside beach not far from my house. For just a few pennies, I could sunbathe on wooden planks and play volleyball in a nearby field. For another penny, I could eat in the busy café. There were small cabins dotting the beach that could be rented for the day.

As I soaked up the sun that day, an approaching figure blocked the sun's rays. "Do you remember me?" the voice said. I looked up at the shadowy figure and replied, "Yes. You are George Kemeny." The two of us then talked about people we both knew and I told him how I had wanted to be a doctor but that law school was more affordable.

The next day it rained. As I was cleaning my brother's apartment that day, my father stopped by to tell me that there was a doctor waiting for me at home. I suspected it might be George and I was right. When I arrived back home, I found George sitting in our dining room, regaling my mother about my intelligence, beauty, and good nature.

The following day the weather had cleared and I invited George to spend the day with me at my uncle's large estate. On the way there, George abruptly asked, "Would you like to go with me to Shanghai?" Many German Jews were fleeing Europe and moving to a Jewish ghetto in Shanghai. I said, "Yes, but neither of us has any money, so we can't." George replied, "Then we are engaged! I was afraid to ask you to marry me." He pulled out a large gold wedding band. I slipped the oversized ring onto my necklace and wore it that way during the seven months that we were engaged.

Before we met, there were rumors that Slovak money would soon be worth nothing and that the government might recall all printed currency. People started buying gold and jewelry to preserve their wealth. George had invested two hundred crowns, the equivalent of two dollars, to buy two of the largest gold wedding rings that he could afford.

After we were engaged, George told me that he had a premonition he would marry a woman from Michalovce. While in medical school, he asked every young female medical student if she was from Michalovce. After he became a doctor, he gave up the notion, then in 1939, during his two-year compulsory service in the Slovak army, he was transferred to Michalovce. His hope that his life partner might be near was renewed, and soon after, George and I met.

*George Kemeny in 1939 during his service
in the Slovak Army.*

CHAPTER FIVE

Life with George

George was one of three sons born to Jolan Haas and Sigmund Kemeny. He was born in Tvrdosin, Slovakia, but his family moved frequently because his father's position as the head of the Slovakia's internal revenue service required it. His older brother, Mikulas, was a very good lawyer who was writing books on finance law under a pseudonym. Mikulas was also a partisan, a member of an insurgent group of Slovak nationals who were rebelling against Slovakia's fascist regime. Like George, his younger brother, Vavro ("Lori"), was also a doctor. Lori lived in Nitra, Slovakia, a town about fifty miles east of Bratislava. Although Lori was not as good a student as George, he was very creative. He was a gifted artist—a self-taught painter who also "had a good pen," as we would say. Lori would eventually leave medicine to become a dentist, so that he would have more time to devote to his painting.

When World War II broke out, George was sent to the border of Poland as part of the medical corps. While he was there he stayed at an inn where many

German soldiers were staying. By this time, the Nuremberg Laws of 1935 were in effect in Poland, one of which forbid social contact between Aryans and Jews. When the owner of the inn said to George, "Doctor, please come down and eat with us," George replied, "No, it would be *rassenschande*[1]. I cannot come down because I am a Jew."

Upset, the innkeeper said to him, "You know, nobody asked me if I am a Jew or Gentile in the First World War and Jews gave me food to eat and a place to stay." Aware of the fascist laws, George insisted, "No, I cannot." The innkeeper finally said, "Then I will bring supper to you."

A few days later the Slovak army demoted George from a lieutenant to an enlisted man. Several weeks later, he was sent home to Bratislava, where he lived with his parents.

To be closer to George, I went to stay with Ilonka in Trencin, which was about a two-hour train ride from Bratislava. One day, George arrived at my sister's home to take me to meet his parents. He was wearing a warm winter suit that his mother had bought for him. My sister's cleaning lady met George at the door. She took one look at George's suit, then looked back at my sister and said, "Don't let Miss Esther go with this man. He is crazy for wearing such a warm suit in August." Hearing this comment, George did not say

---

[1] racial defilement

to me, "My mother bought me that suit. They did not have other suits, and she was thinking about winter." Instead, he quipped, "This suit keeps the heat in and the cold out. So I'm warm if it's cold out and cool if it's warm out."

An hour into the train ride to Bratislava, I told George if his mother looks at us disapprovingly, I wouldn't go in. After meeting his parents, I was pleased when his mother said to me, "I was afraid of whom George would bring home, but today a stone has fallen off my heart."

From that moment on, I was warmly accepted into his family.

Tvrdosin, Slovakia.
Birthplace of George Kemeny.

George, Lori, and Mikulas Kemeny.

In 1939, when Hitler's regime reached Slovakia, my father wanted to move his family to America. He applied to the consulate for his U.S. citizenship and got a joint passport photo taken with my mother. Just as they were preparing for the move, my mother fell ill with cancer. Then, in February of 1940, her doctor came to me and said, "Your mother will not be here for more than two or three days. You should get married now so that she can see her last child marry."

A law required couples to be married in a civil ceremony. Before the ceremony, an announcement of the nuptials was posted and a waiting period was in effect. This allowed anyone who objected to the union an opportunity to come forward. Under the circumstances, George and I chose not to wait. Because our rabbi was bound by the law, an assistant rabbi agreed to marry us.

The next day, my father assembled a *minyan*[2] in our dining room and George and I stood under the *hupah*, the Jewish bridal canopy. My mother was propped up in her bed and the French doors dividing the bedroom from the dining room were opened. She looked at George and me and smiled. She seemed very happy.

Before the wedding, George had my engagement ring resized to fit my finger. We did not have any

---

[2] a prayer quorum of ten men

money, but in his pocket he had a small dowry to spend and asked me if I preferred to receive a pocketbook or a bouquet of flowers. I chose the pocketbook because I did not have one. Three days later, on Wednesday, February 24, 1940, my mother died. She was sixty-four years old. The trains had not been running for several days because of heavy snowfall, so George's parents and Ilonka were not able to attend either my wedding or my mother's funeral.

My father was devastated by my mother's death. He wrote my mother's name in his bible and cried. I tried to soothe him but he said, "Nothing else is left for me. The person I love most is gone," then added, "Now I will save you." Three weeks later, my seventy-one-year-old father left for America by himself with a plan to get his children to America.

In order for us to be granted American passports, my father first had to be on American soil. Three weeks after he set sail from Italy, he arrived in the U.S. Upon his arrival, he stayed in Brooklyn, New York, with one of his brothers whom he had not seen in forty-five years.

As soon as my father's feet touched American soil, my siblings and I were called to the American Consulate in Budapest to apply for our American passports.

*The 1939 joint passport photo of
Josephine and Max Berkowitz.*

Esther and George Kemeny.

As we waited for our passports to be issued, Nazi momentum in Slovakia reached a critical mass. Many Jews were trying to flee Slovakia. In Bratislava, there was a boat taking Jewish children to Israel. My family wanted my mother's wealthy cousin, Max Brügler ("Uncle Miscka"), to sponsor ten children for the journey. The trip cost three thousand crowns, or thirty dollars, per child. My uncle, who was known to be stingy, declined to participate. He said he needed the money for himself. Ultimately, Uncle Miscka's money did not serve him. During the war he was taken to a concentration camp, where he died.

In July of 1940, Hitler issued a directive to intensify anti-Semitic actions in Slovakia. The following month, a law requiring the registration of all Jewish property in Slovakia was enacted and the Judenkodex Ordinance, which deprived Slovak Jews of many basic freedoms, was passed. By September, laws for the Aryanization of Slovakia were in effect.

It was through these laws that my wealthy uncle, Bernard Berkowitz, had his thousand-acre plot of land taken from him and the acreage divided among the peasants. Two years later my uncle was taken to a concentration camp. Neither he nor his wife and children survived the war.

On June 13, 1941, my siblings and I were issued our passports but our spouses' applications for visas were denied. Even though America's President Roosevelt was aware of the persecution of Jews in Europe, his administration was prohibiting the issuance of visas.

After my three brothers were issued their passports, they left for the United States from Lisbon, Portugal. Icu was thirty-nine years old; Ari, thirty-three; and Sanyi, thirty-one. At the time, Icu and Ari were married and hopeful that they would be able to get their wives out of Slovakia in the near future. But reality proved to be far different from their expectations.

Ilonka and I decided to stay in Slovakia. Both of us were recently wed and did not want to be separated from our husbands. During our discussion about my leaving, George said, "We do not know how long this war will last. We married for better and for worse. The two of us should be together. Whatever happens, happens."

At the time, we were living near the Ukraine, but had seen no military action. We had heard of the *Einsatzgruppen* and Auschwitz, and knew there were other concentration camps, but we knew nothing about their precise nature.

After my siblings left for America, George's father, who was well-known and highly regarded in Bratislava, used his influence to get George got a job as an intern in a hospital in Michalovce. There, George earned two or three dollars a month. Because they knew that George was not making much money, some patients gave George tips. At the time, we were living in my parents' home, but still, George worried about being able to support us. He knew that his boss was a fascist.

After three months' employment, George was dismissed from the hospital. We then moved to Bratislava where George found a job digging ditches. One day at the ministry, his father mentioned that his son needed a job. From this, George was placed in a hospital in Ruzomberok, a town in central Slovakia about four hours from Bratislava. Again, after three months, George was let go from the hospital. During that time, I went to live with George's parents. I thought that I needed to learn a practical trade in case we immigrated to another country since it seemed unlikely that a doctorate degree from a Slovak university would be recognized abroad, so I enrolled in a course to learn how to sew men's shirts and pajamas and women's lingerie. My teacher was Zoli Farkas's sister.

While I was living with my in-laws, I came down with walking pneumonia. I perspired so much that I needed to change my nightgown two or three times during the night. To help cure me, Jolan gave me boiled wine to drink.

Later, Jolan had purchased some black silk fabric so that I could make a slip for her. Zoli's sister helped me by cutting out the material. When Zoli's sister left me alone for a few moments to go to the store, I decided to prove to her that I could sew a straight line. In doing so, I accidentally cut off a whole piece of material. When I had finished, there was no room left in the slip for Jolan's breasts and hips.

When Zoli's sister returned from the store, she took one look at my handiwork and snapped, "Go and buy more material. We will have to add some slits to expand the slip." When we were done, I presented two slips to Jolan: the one that we had salvaged and another one that I had sewn correctly. To save face, when I presented the slips to Jolan, I told her a little white lie: I asked her to try on both slips because I wanted to see which style she preferred.

After George was released from Ruzomberok, his father got him a residency in a hospital in Zvolen, a city in western Slovakia, where George seemed to flourish. His boss loved him because he was a good doctor. George was earning three dollars a month plus the extra money that patients gave to him in tips. About this time, the first transports to concentration camps in Slovakia had begun. All unmarried Jewish girls were being sent off to the camps. Ari's wife,

Stephanie, had a beautiful younger sister that we wanted to save. We introduced her to one of the surgeons in the hospital in Zvolen. Right after they were married, they went into hiding with Stephanie's parents and her younger brother. Stephanie remained in Bratislava and went into hiding on her own.

Stephanie's family had a good deal of American money and jewelry, including diamonds. To hide it from the Nazis, they sewed all of it into the lining of her father's coat. Shortly thereafter, the Germans discovered them. Stephanie's parents, her younger brother, her sister, and her brother-in-law all were shot and killed. I do not know if the coat was ever found; if it was, the new owner is now wealthy.

Two years after he began working in Zvolen, George was dismissed from the hospital. He quickly got a new position in a hospital in Levoca, a city in eastern Slovakia, but was very unhappy there. Again, he answered to a fascist. Because I was not allowed to live in the hospital, I lived in a rented a room right across the street. George would bring food over to my room and we would eat our meals together.

In 1943, George contracted scarlet fever and was quarantined in the hospital. From my exposure to him, I became infected with strep throat. My landlady was so frightened by my illness that she refused to enter my room to place logs on the fire or to feed me. Luckily, a friend of ours, Magda Rector, the wife of George's colleague, Dr. Rector, brought some food to me during my illness.

When George and I had both recovered, George was allowed to join me in my room once more. As we continued to share time in our little room together we hoped something would happen soon to end the war.

Concern over George's suffering at the hands his fascist boss prompted my father-in-law to use his influence to intervene. George was then transferred to a hospital in Topolcany, a town about sixty miles east of Bratislava. By this time, the Slovak government was in dire need of doctors. Because of this, hospitals were loath to dismiss Jewish doctors. However, they did not want their patients to know that Jews were taking care of them, so George and I were not required to wear the yellow star insignia on our clothes that identified us as Jews.

George and I lived inside the hospital in Topolcany in a small room that had a single bed and a divan. We alternated months sleeping on the divan and it worked out very well. By then, laws were in effect forbidding Jews to be in public places. Among the restrictions, Jews could not go to the park or see a movie. Although George and I did not have to wear the yellow star insignia, we did not leave the hospital because we did not want participate in the fascist society.

In late August 1944, Slovak nationals, including George's brother, Mikulas, staged an uprising against the fascist regime in Banska Bystrica, a town near Zvolen. The uprising lasted about five days. Ultimately, the Germans crushed the rebellion and Mikulas was killed for being a partisan. His widow put their three children in a cloister where nuns looked after them and kept them out of harm's way by hiding them in the cellar whenever Germans approached. By this time, George's father had suffered a fatal heart attack and Jolan was also living in the hospital in Topolcany.

In September, several days after the brunt of the uprising in Banska Bystrica, the Germans came to the hospital in Topolcany looking for Jewish doctors. I was three months pregnant and lying down in my room because I was not feeling well. The Germans stormed in and told us to "Pack and go." I showed a German officer my American passport. He spit on it and took it away.

One day before, George's boss offered to hide us in his parents' home. But George said to him, "I cannot betray my Jewish colleagues. I have already told them that I did not have a place to hide. I cannot go back on my words." George's mother had also declined protection. A friend of hers who was a

Catholic priest offered to take her in. She told him, "They will come for my children. I cannot leave them behind. I must be with them."

*Standing: Priest who offered to hide Jolan, George.
Sitting: Wife of the hospital administrator, Esther, and Jolan.*

CHAPTER SIX

Sered

We were taken to the railroad station, escorted by huge guard dogs. George was carrying a suitcase filled with some of our belongings, including a roll of salami that we had saved. When we arrived at the station, we did not know where we were going. We were put on a cattle car along with others. About two hours later, we arrived at Camp Sered, one of Slovakia's largest labor camps. The camp was on a military base. The Germans housed us in military barracks; twenty of us were placed in a space designed for eight. Jolan, George, and I were able to remain together. We were allowed to keep our own clothes and the Jewish community in the camp made sure we had food to eat. Slovak fascist soldiers were in charge of guarding us. They locked us in the barracks every night at eight o'clock. At night, when they were drunk and wanted to amuse themselves, they woke us up, chased us out of the barracks into the square, and beat us with whips. During these brutal episodes, they killed up to three men each night. The soldiers were not shooting women, so whenever we were driven out into the square at night, Jolan and I sheltered George by encircling him.

We stayed at Camp Sered until the Germans had transported twelve- to fifteen hundred people into the camp. Four weeks later they met their quota. They crammed us into ten cattle wagons and took us by train to Auschwitz. During the journey, we could not see out of the cars. No food or water was given to us. People ate whatever they happened to have with them; George had taken our salami. There were no toilets in the cattle cars. People were forced to soil themselves or relieve themselves on the cattle car floor.

Auschwitz

We arrived in Auschwitz on October 17, 1944, in the dark hours of early morning. As soon as we stepped off the train, the Germans separated the men from the women by ordering all of the men to go in one direction and all of the women to go in another. We were then lined up in rows of five. I stood alongside Jolan and Mrs. Lowenger, the wife of a physician friend, and their three-year-old son.

Dr. Mengele was in charge of selections. He ordered Mrs. Lowenger, her son, and Jolan to one side and they were led away. I said to Dr. Mengele, "That's my mother" and asked if I could join her. He said,

"Don't worry, you will see her in the morning."

In the morning, what I saw was a gas chamber and a crematorium. I realized then that Jolan and the Lowengers had been sent to their deaths. Jolan was killed one day before her fifty-third birthday.

After the war, I was told that Dr. Lowenger, upon hearing the fate of his family, had thrown himself onto the electrified wire fence that surrounded the camp.

Because Dr. Mengele considered me one of "healthy people," that is, an able-bodied worker, I was not sent to the gas chamber but to the "shower room," a large room where water dripped from ceiling. There, I was stripped naked and my head was shaved and my glasses and my ring were taken away from me. I was then given wooden clogs and a short-sleeved summer dress to wear, but no undergarments. My dress was several sizes too small for me: its length fell well above my knees. They tattooed my arm and assigned me to the *Zigeunerlager*, or Gypsy barracks, where earlier the Germans had killed many Gypsies.

When we arrived, it was the middle of October and already quite cold and rainy. Winters in Poland are severe. While in Auschwitz, my shoes and feet were always wet because we were always walking in snow and water; yet, during my time in Auschwitz, I never caught a cold.

Roll call was held every morning at five outside of the barracks in the middle of the camp courtyard. During roll call we had to stand outside for two or three hours in the freezing cold waiting for the SS women to finish counting all of us. During my first roll call, I was weak from hunger and fainted. I fell face-first into the mud. At Auschwitz, we were never given any water to drink or wash up in, so that mud remained on my face until the end of the war.

Jewish overseers, called *kapos*, were in charge of us prisoners. They gave orders in German but also spoke Yiddish and Polish. They told us that the Germans were gassing and burning twelve hundred people a day and warned us not to be caught in the barracks during the day or we, too, would be gassed. They emphasized that we must follow all orders given to us.

Most of the prisoners left the camp each day to work outside of the camp. I was put to work in the kitchen. Several of us were assigned to peeling potatoes. Every day, all day, from seven or eight in the morning to four in the afternoon, we had to peel enough potatoes to feed the thousands and thousands of people at the camp. The kettle that needed to be filled was the size of a small room. We were not permitted to talk as we worked. Rather than allow us to eat the peels, the cruel overseers made us throw them into the latrine. Many times out of hunger I fished out the peels from the feces-filled latrine and ate them.

When we returned to the barracks at the end of a workday, we were fed a bowl of watery potato soup and a piece of bread—our entire rations for the day. I was not issued a bowl of my own, so I had to wait until others were finished eating before I could have my portion. By then, the soup was nearly gone and my soup rarely had any potatoes in it.

On Christmas Eve, we were given two portions of bread with our soup. I wanted to save that extra portion of bread for later, but there were too many rats running around eager to take our food, so instead I decided to eat it.

The prisoners slept on wooden bunks. I was issued a coarse, thin horse blanket that was infested with lice. Even though I was exhausted from working all day without enough food, it was difficult to sleep at night because of the cold and the intense itching from the lice. Without my glasses, I could not see the lice, but tried to remove them just the same. I kept my wet wooden shoes on even while I slept, to prevent them from being stolen.

Jews were not the only ones who were sent to Auschwitz. In addition to the Gypsies, other targets included homosexuals, Polish women from the Warsaw uprising, and other Germans. One day I said to one of the little German girls at camp, "I know why I am here, but why are you here?" She said that one day she cut her hand at work and did not go to work the next day because her hand hurt. Because she did not show up for work, they sent her to Auschwitz.

Everyone in the barracks was friendly to each other, but we were too tired and depressed to talk. All of us were hungry, cold, apathetic, and thought "what will be, will be."

I prayed that the Allies would bombard the camp at night, but they never did. When I looked around, there was nothing to see but the gas chamber and the crematorium. The air always smelled of burning flesh. When they burned the bodies, I could see the smoke rising from the crematorium. The Germans kept what they were doing so quiet that nobody outside the camps knew what was going on. Escape seemed impossible. There was one guard for every five prisoners. Armed SS soldiers with dogs guarded the perimeter of the camp and the barbed-wire fences were electrified. I heard of no one successfully escaping the camp, with the exception of one young man, who went to Budapest and wrote to Roosevelt and Pope Pius XII to tell them what was going on.

Since the moment we had arrived at Auschwitz, I did not know where George was or even if he was alive. My hope and feeling that I would one day see him again pulled me through my ordeal. I was fat when I entered the camp and mentally strong. If I were any thinner, or if they knew that I was pregnant, I believe they would have gassed me for sure.

One December evening, I came back to barracks in the snow, nearly naked. After I ate my soup and bread, I lay down on the bunk. Moments later, I heard the Polish women singing carols. "It must be Christmas," I said. Just as I said that, I felt my baby give a little kick. I was five months pregnant. That same night, I felt a terrible pain in my abdomen. A Polish woman took me to the infirmary. I went into labor and gave birth to a little boy. Afterwards, the bleeding did not stop. I bled for two hours over a bedpan before a doctor was called. When the doctor arrived, with unwashed hands, she pulled out the placenta. Then the Polish woman threw my baby in the garbage, where he died.

I lamented, "Where is my God? If we are the chosen people, why do we have to suffer so much?" Still, I prayed. I did not believe that God punishes those he loves.

Before I returned to the barracks, the doctor urged me to get up for roll call. If I was found in the barracks during roll call, I would be gassed.

I lay on my wooden bunk for awhile unable to sleep. The lice were itching, the rats were running all over me, and the roll call hour was approaching. After enduring roll call, I was assigned to work in the children's hospitals, where I looked after small Russian children who were suffering from diarrhea. Part of my job was to haul large barrels of feces to the latrine with another woman. Many times we slipped and fell and the feces splashed our faces and clothes. Since I had no water to wash up in, I did not smell like roses.

When I returned to the barracks, I was cold, wet, and shivering. I ate my daily ration and sat down on my bunk. I felt worse than ever. I was alone without my baby. When I prayed, I felt empty; there was no one to answer back with his kicks anymore.

Days came and went and I continued to come and go like a robot. To stave off hunger, I cooked all of the time in my head. There were no distractions. There was nothing to read and no paper on which to write. The only music in camp was played by a band of prisoners—musicians forced to serenade those headed to their deaths in the gas chamber.

To survive, I focused on getting through each hour of every day. I could not sleep because of my depression, but I never lost my will to live. I wanted to live, even with the knowledge that there were very cruel people in the world.

The Death March

Three weeks after the birth and death of my baby, in mid-January 1945, the Germans told everyone that they were going to blow up Auschwitz and that we should pack and go. The Germans gave me a pair of shoes and I made myself a pair of pants out of blankets.

The day before the march, a fifteen-year-old girl came to me crying and said, "I was selected to go to the crematorium; they chose my number." I told her, "Listen. Perhaps there will not be a crematorium tomorrow. Maybe we will survive." She was only skin and bones at the time. I do not know if she survived.

The march started on January 17, 1945, and lasted five days. During the march, we had to run for three days without any food or water. As we ran, we saw dead men on the side of every road. The guards kept yelling, "*Schnell! Schnell!*" which meant, "Faster! Faster!" A physician friend, who about ten years older than I, told me she could not make it and had to stop. She stopped for a moment and was shot dead on the side of the road.

The SS had their dogs and machine guns turned on us at all times. The SS were not soldiers; they were killers. After three days of running, a train took us the rest of the way to Ravensbrück, a camp in Germany.

Ravensbrück

At Ravensbrück, they were not prepared for us and gave us no food to eat. I heard that a new transport from Czechoslovakia was arriving. George's cousin and a woman from Michalovce were in the transport. They had been given some soup and potatoes to eat. George's cousin told me that they were afraid to eat the soup because they had diarrhea, and asked me if I wanted some. I said, "Sure." By that time, I had not eaten in four or five days. I went to the barracks to get a container for the soup. A lady gave me a half-gallon milk can. I promised her I would share the soup with her, but the soup was so warm and so satisfying that I could not help but drink it all up.

Two days later, we were put on an open coal train. When we arrived at Neustadt-Glewe, a sub-camp of Ravensbrück, more than half of the people on the train had frozen to death.

CHAPTER SEVEN

Liberation

Neustadt-Glewe was just like Auschwitz. Every morning there was roll call and we were given the same meager rations. I wore a flimsy dress and shoes because my other clothes were stolen while I was in Ravensbrück. Immediately after I arrived, I was put to work building bunkers for the German airplanes. I dug ditches all day long at gunpoint.

While it was uncommon for a German soldier to show humanity, one day a guard from the German Air Force gave me hope by telling me that war would be over soon because the Germans were running out of fuel for their airplanes.

On the evening of May 2, 1945, we heard a hammer-like pounding on the barracks door. The Germans were locking us in the barracks by nailing pieces of wood across the door and the windows. At dawn the next morning, there was a loud banging on the door. A Russian woman with an axe in her hand burst into the barracks and cried, "We are free!" In the middle of the night, the Germans had fled.

The wires separating the camp from the German Air Force barracks next door were cut with the axe and the Russian women told us to go get some cereal at the Air Force facility, where there were two huge kettles of cereal were waiting for us. The cereal was still warm when I ate it.

I remained scared. I believed that the Germans would return. I found several raw potatoes and put them under my blanket. I sat on them all day, waiting for the Germans to return.

The Russians gave us twenty-four hours to plunder the city for food and clothes, but during that time I was too frightened to leave the barracks. Throughout the day, I watched other prisoners bringing food and clothes back to the barracks. Some of the prisoners did not leave the barracks because they were too ill from hunger to move. Their legs were swollen from starvation-induced edema.

The following day, I dared to go into the city—not for myself—but to find food for three women with swollen legs. As I walked up one street, I came to a corner, where a twenty-gallon can of milk sat in front of a house. I went inside of the house to inquire about the milk, where I was met by three Russian soldiers. I asked them if I could have some of the milk. They said yes, but that they would first feed some of it to the dog to make sure it had not been poisoned. They warned me that the twenty-four-hour plunder period had expired and martial law was now in effect.

I told them about the three starving women back at the barracks and one soldier offered to help me take some food back to them. He brought a child's small red wagon from behind the house and we walked to a nearby house where a young pregnant woman and her father lived. The soldier asked them where their pantry was. When they told him that they did not have one, he went down to their cellar, where there were all kinds of food—preserved chickens and geese and jars of fruit. We took a chicken preserved in fat and a few jars of fruit.

Later that afternoon when I made another trip into the city, I noticed many prisoners coming and going from one particular house, so I went inside it. In the bedroom there was a dresser with a mirror. I was afraid to look at myself. I looked just like a bad boy. My hair was just growing in and I had mud and feces caked all over my face. On the dresser there was a bottle of *4711* cologne. I thought I could wash my face with it, so I took the bottle. A friend who saw me take it pulled me aside and said, "Listen, the lady sitting there is the owner of the house." I felt ashamed that I had taken the cologne right in front of her and put it back on the dresser.

I walked up to the woman and said, "May I ask a favor of you? May I have a warm bath and a clean pair of clothes?" She replied, "Sure, come with me to the woodshed," where we gathered wood to build a fire to warm the water for my bath. When I was finished bathing, I burned my old clothes in the bathroom stove. The woman offered me some clean clothes and a pair of stockings and shoes. I felt like a person again.

She also gave me a man's gabardine coat and a typewriter. She thought I could shorten the coat for my husband. I did not want to seem ungrateful, so I took them both. As I was leaving her house a Russian soldier looked at the typewriter and asked, "*musika?*" thinking I was carrying an accordion. I said, "Yes," and handed him the heavy typewriter. I later gave the large coat to a friend.

When I returned to the barracks, the Russians were waiting to take us to Prenzlau, Germany, where we were concentrated before being sent home on buses. During the first week there, we were with Belgian prisoners of war. The soldiers gave us some soap and water and Red Cross chocolates, and one officer gave me a nice Eisenhower jacket. I made a skirt made from a gray blanket and sewed a blouse from a gingham tablecloth. Before they were flown back to Belgium, I gave the addresses of my father and my brothers in America to one of the officers. He told me that he would write to them to tell them that I was alive.

Prenzlau

After three or four weeks, the first transport bus arrived at Prenzlau, but we learned it was reserved for the women of Lidice.

Lidice was a small mining village in Bohemia that the Germans razed in vengeance in 1942 because they believed the townsfolk helped kill the German Nazi police general, Reinhard Heydrich. Before they set fire to the town, the Germans shot all of the nearly two hundred men of Lidice and took all of the town's women to Ravensbrück. A few of the children were sent away for "re-education" and adopted into German families; the others were taken to extermination camps.

After we were informed that the first bus would not be taking us home, I was given a scrap piece of paper and told to write down my name, my husband's name, exactly where I was taken from, and the message that I was alive and waiting for transportation home. I was told that this information was going to be broadcast on the radio. When I wrote this note, I still did not know if George was dead or alive.

The message was never broadcast on the radio; instead, it was sent to the hospital in Topolcany from where George, Jolan, and I were taken. Four weeks after it was sent, George received the news that I was

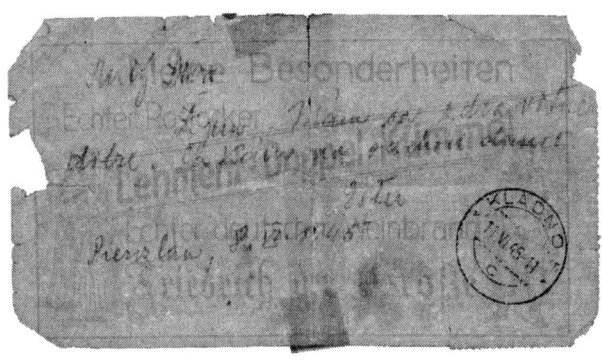

*Esther's handwritten message to George sent from Prenzlau.
(front and back)*

alive. Until then, he was traveling once a week to Topolcany to see if there was any news from me.

While in Prenzlau, I met up with the wife of an older doctor from Topolcany. Her husband and she had been taken to the camps at the same time as George and I. She was wearing men's shoes, one black and one brown, and in her hands was an egg slicer.

I asked her why, so many weeks after liberation, was she wearing those shoes. She said that she had not been feeling well for awhile, then went where the Belgian officers were staying and found the shoes. When I asked her why she had took an egg slicer, she said, "It was the only thing left to take."

Her husband did not survive the camps.

Prague

In June 1945, after eight weeks in Prenzlau, a bus came for us and took us to Prague. When we arrived, the Red Cross put us up in a school and gave us food to eat. We were instructed to go the Ministry of Health to determine if we had any contagious diseases. As I was leaving the ministry building after my check up, I saw a familiar face at the bottom of the stairs. I recognized him as a physician from Topolcany who was a close associate of George's. But he had changed. His skin was yellow and he was very thin. I said, "Karol, do you have any information about George?" He replied, "Yes. George died in my arms." My heart sank. I walked back to the school, crying.

After a terrible sleepless night, I returned to the ministry the next day to obtain the results of my blood tests. When I reached the building, I saw George's colleague standing at the bottom of stairs, exactly where I met him the day before. I said to him, "Karol, please tell me, how did George die?" He said, "George did not die. He was taken by transport to Stettin." I realized then that he was disturbed, but now I had hope.

On the street, I met a lawyer friend, Dr. Benes, the nephew of President Benes. When he asked me how I was doing, I started to cry and said to him, "I do not know anything about my husband. I believe he might have been transported to Stettin." He said, "I am going to look for the women from Lidice. Give me some information on George. If he is alive, I will find him." Later that day, I ran into Dr. Rector, the psychiatrist friend whose wife, Magda, had helped me in Levoca when I was sick. I asked, "How is Magda?" He replied, "She's fine. And how is George?" Again, I broke down and cried. I told him I did not know if he was dead or alive. He quickly said, "Don't you know, Esther? George was nominated *primarius*[3] of internal medicine at a hospital in Rimavská Sobota." He said that Lori was a resident in the hospital in Kosice and that the UNRRA (United Nations Relief and Rehabilitation Agency) truck was leaving his hotel at five the next morning to take him to Kosice. I asked if I could go with him. He said, "Certainly, but how will you manage to get to the hotel on time? The last streetcar is at midnight."

"I will take the midnight run to the hotel and sleep on the steps of the hotel or on a park bench. I have slept in worse places."

I went back to the school. A short time later, while I was at the Red Cross station eating lunch, a woman from the Red Cross rushed over to me and said, "Hurry, hurry! Dr. Rector just called. They are not leaving tomorrow, but this afternoon at two o'clock."

On my bed back at the school I had three hundred crowns, a ticket to Bratislava, and a lunchbox that the Red Cross had given me. There was not enough time to go back and get them. I rushed to the hotel with nothing but the clothes on my back and the bar of chocolate in my coat pocket.

Dr. Rector paid my five-hundred-crown fare for the trip. On the way to Kosice, we stayed overnight in Silesia, where he paid for my room in a hotel and gave me a comb and a toothbrush.

[3] chief

Kosice

We arrived in Kosice around eleven at night. Dr. Rector had advised me not to go to a hotel because he had heard that the Russians were raping women there, so I went straight to the hospital where Lori was working. At the hospital, I rang the doorbell and the doorman came out.

I said, "I am looking for Dr. Kemeny." We went inside. The doorman looked up and down his list of names. All sorts of Slovak names were on it, but no Kemeny. I asked the doorman for directions to the doctors' quarters, where I was met by an old friend, Dr. Kurty. I told him of my plans to go to Rimavská Sobota the next day to see George and asked him if I could sleep on the hospital ward floor overnight. He looked at me puzzled and said, "Why do you want to sleep on the floor when your brother-in-law is here? Why not sleep on one of the beds in his room?" When I told him that Lori's name was not on the list of the doctors, he said that George and Lori had changed their last name to Oravec on the advice of Dr. Turso, the minister of health and a former classmate of George's. Dr. Turso was the one who had nominated George for the esteemed position at Rimavská Sobota. He had told George, "You are the first Jew nominated for this position because you were such a good student in medical school and are such a good doctor. No one will object to your nomination. However, you must not have a Hungarian-sounding name."

Lori and George chose the name Oravec because Orava was the county in which they were born. Other doctors with Hungarian surnames, including Dr. Kurty, had also changed their names.

As I was talking with Dr. Kurty, Lori came walking towards us. When he saw me, he pinched himself. He could not believe I was standing before him.

I learned from Lori that George and he were in the camps together until they were liberated. Lori had been deported to Auschwitz from Nitra. When he arrived at Auschwitz, he was sent to a barracks in the same part of the camp as George. Lori began looking for George and soon found him in George's barracks. While he was visiting George's barracks, the Germans had transported all of the men from Lori's barracks out of the camp, so Lori stayed with George.

They were in Auschwitz for only two days before they were transported to Friedland, on the border of Silesia, to work in the concentration camp of Gross-Rosen. There, they worked on airplane wings. George deliberately sabotaged the planes by not putting in all of the parts.

Because George and Lori did not stay at Auschwitz very long, they were not tattooed. During their internment, neither of them revealed that they were doctors. They did not want to be forced to perform experiments on people or select people for the gas chamber. Gross-Rosen was close to the Czechoslovak border, so they were able to return home right after liberation.

Then Lori informed me that George was not in Rimavská Sobota but at a university hospital in Bratislava. The hospital in Rimavská Sobota turned George away when they found out he was a Jew.

For the next several days, I sent George telegrams to let him know that I was coming to him. Two days later he responded: "I am waiting for you."

It took three days to reach Bratislava by train because the bridges had been destroyed during the bombardments. On the train ride, I met a friend from Michalovce who offered to put me up for the night in her home in Bratislava.

Lori's sketches from Auschwitz.

CHAPTER EIGHT

Finding George

At dawn the next morning, I began to search for George. Bratislava was a big city of over 300,000 people. I knew he was at the university hospital, but I had no idea how to get there. I thought his cousin might know, so I walked over to her place. I arrived at her door around six in the morning. She did not know where George was, but thought that a friend of George's, Dr. Strauss, might know. I walked over to Dr. Strauss' home and he was able to help me.

Around seven in the morning, I arrived at the hospital. I found George sitting in the hospital dining room eating his breakfast. When he saw me, he gasped, "My god, we almost missed each other!"

The day before, in his eagerness to see me, he went to the UNRRA truck driver and asked him how much it would cost to go to Kosice. The driver told him five hundred crowns. George only had three hundred crowns, so he could not make the trip.

Our reunion was both joyful and bittersweet. George had hoped that our child survived my ordeal. Before he knew of my fate, he wrote letters to me in a journal every day:

On the Shores of Darkness

"Esterl, my beloved come back to me!

Can you know how beautiful it will be when you
return? We shall take walks into the woods.
Under our feet there will be a carpet of moss and
fir needles. In the air the birds will sing, and the
pines will surround us with their fragrance. We
shall hold hands and run a little. Only we, the two
of us alone, no one else will see us. What a joy it
will be. And we'll come to a lake, with a boat
waiting for us. From the sky—or heaven?—the
sunshine will pour down on us in a flood. And
I'll sit down close to you, my dear soul, in the boat.
We will keep silent, looking quietly in the distance.
You will be dressed in bright colors. Flowers of
the field will be in your hair. And all around us
the silence will be glorious. Only the angels from
heaven will smile down on us and over the waves
and the breeze to play for us the melody of
unending love. And we shall remain long, very long
above all, only ourselves, from the shores listening
to mysterious and beautiful sounds. We won't look
at each other. So we don't wound our hearts by
seeing our faces from which perhaps the shadows
of horror so recent can never fade away. But I
know, my dear Esterl, that when at twilight's
dim light, I take a timid, furtive glance at you,
your face will not only be grave and sad, but
will radiate joy and have a glimmer of a happy
smile. You will be all beautiful to me. That's how
I would like to see you. Sadly serious, devotedly
happy, the mouth suggesting a light and perhaps
somewhat pain-filled smile, the face telling the
fullness of your compassion and understanding.
That's how I'll know you, my soul yearns, longs

for you in all my dreams. You are the sun and shine of my love, my soul mate in so many of my sorrows and sufferings. Only come back, please. It's a promise, isn't it. Thank you. I love you very much. Come back!"

George

"My Esterl, my only one, my beloved wife,

My heart is full with deep thanks that God listened to my call and liberated me from slavery. My heart was beating hard when I returned to my country, to the country which I love, where the people are near to me, even if they—blinded with the curse of evil—threw me out. I hope that I will be able to embrace you, my soul, nearest and dearest to me. A little spark of hope that you gave a gift to me, of a little angelic soul, of which—do you remember my sweet wife? We were praying with trust. In the work and tiredness of slavery, I saw your sad and serious eyes. I heard your warm voice, when I worked for consolation in misery and anxiety among the noise of machines, and in this sorrow, your hands were caressing mine. Believe me, I did not know that we were so bonded! My Esterl, do I have to repeat how I love you? Do I have to say that I am longing for you? That I love you more than at anytime before? It hurts me if I was sometimes not very loving to you. In our happy love, we had only very hard times together. Unhappiness was accompanying us. I am not complaining. Maybe our understanding and remembering, which made me happy, was the result of the big secret of suffering. It seems that we have a difficult time ahead of us. If I would have learned how to pray, I would be scared even to think of your hard labor. In the camp you are carrying the fruit of our love, a big gift of the Almighty. You are always walking in peril of life. There are many tears of fear in my eyes. We are weak, and the enemy is cruel and strong. And there is a pain in my chest. My soul called, "Help me God! Take care of me and my people!" I am again hopeful, Esterl, my love. Esterl, my love, separated, we had to continue with our life. The life is hard in freedom, harder than in the camp. Where are you, my soul? I don't know even if you are alive. Where are you, my love? Do you think of me? I hope that you are somewhere with our baby, on which you look with your sad eyes. I see how you look lovingly at our child whom you are holding near your heart. For now I don't have you near. My happiness is not yet fulfilled. We did not reach the bottom of the chalice. For a moment I am happy. I cannot imagine that we won't have children. I love you my sweet soul. The doubt is so terrible. I will be very good to you—supporting and loving—I promise you, when you return. Please return my love with our gift. Return, my sweetheart, with our beautiful flower. We will bring up our child who will be full of peace and love. I think very often of our meeting. Will we be happy or cry that we are together again? What will we say first? We won't need words. We understand each other without talking. You will look into my eyes. Your eyes will be maybe sadder. There will be few words, and then we'll embrace. There will be tears in your eyes, and then we will look at our gift from God, and after a while, I will take your face into my trembling hand, and I will kiss your cheeks and mouth. I will be the happiest person in this world."

George

CHAPTER NINE

Post-War Life

After our reunion, George and I went to stay with Ilonka. While in Trencin, George had his lungs x-rayed and we discovered he had contracted tuberculosis in the camps. George stayed at a sanatorium in the Tatra Mountains for three weeks. After his release from the sanatorium, he was nominated for a *primarius* position in a hospital in Presov. In Czechoslovakia, the hospitals were run by the government and high-level positions were awarded through a nomination and election process. George was the first Jew to be elected to his new position.

As a *primarius*, he earned a high salary and had three residents and two interns working for him. His staff assisted him in his rounds, which allowed him to take naps during the day until he was fully recovered from his illness. During this period he published research articles in several medical journals and set up a private practice in the hospital in which he saw twenty to thirty patients a day. I concentrated on feeding him well and George began to slowly regain his strength.

During the war, many peasants became squatters.

Esther and George a few weeks after their reunion.

They moved into the cities and took over the homes of the Jews who fled or had been taken away by the Nazis. Because of this, when the war was over, it was difficult to find housing in the cities. George and I could not find a place to live in Presov, so we continued to live in the hospital. It was about this time that I received a tax bill for my Uncle Bernard's estate, the one that the Nazis had seized and divided amongst the peasants. Because I was my uncle's only known living relative, they considered me to be the heir to his estate and liable for the taxes due. The matter was resolved when I convinced them that the estate was decimated during the war and was now in the hands of the peasants.

At the end of 1945, I became pregnant, but lost the baby in my sixth month. Later that year, around Christmas, George and I got a letter and photograph from my father. He was living in The Jewish Home for the Aged in New York, where Ari was the director of accounting. He wrote how happy he was living in the home. He said that he liked to watch people play cards and described a beautiful garden where he enjoyed taking walks.

George looked at the photo of my father that was enclosed with the letter and said, "Your father looks as if he might have had a stroke." One week later, we received a letter from Ari telling us that on the day that we had received my father's letter, my father had died in his sleep. Ari said that on Christmas night, my father was watching others play cards then went to his room to go to sleep. He never woke up.

He closed his letter with, "Father lived like a hero and died like a saint."

In 1946, I lost another baby in the sixth month of pregnancy. In 1947, I became pregnant again and my baby boy was born prematurely seven months later. He lived for just one day. Two days after his birth, I started to have intense pain in my lungs. George suggested that I had pleurisy. When the pain became unbearable, I asked George for a painkiller.

George thought that in my grief for the loss of our baby, I might be suffering from a psychosomatic illness. He gave me an injection that contained no pain reliever. After a sleepless night of pain, the next morning, a hospital worker came in to tidy my room. She held up a full vial of morphine that George had left in the room and asked me what she should do with it. I told her to give it to me and I drank the entire vial.

Soon afterwards, I started to feel good again. When they came in to x-ray me, I told them I was

*Max Berkowitz at the Jewish
Home for the Aged in New York.*

feeling much better and so they let me sleep. Later, I started to spit up blood. George and the other doctors feared that I might have cancer, but x-rays revealed that my lungs were full of blood. George put two and two together and realized that I most likely had suffered a thrombosis in my lung that had burst. I was ordered to stay in bed for six weeks until my lungs had cleared.

In early 1948, the communists took over Czechoslovakia. One day that year, George's friend from the Ministry of Social Services asked us why, after two years, were we still living in the hospital. George explained our predicament. The next day we were granted a beautiful apartment in town that had a kitchen, a bath, three rooms, and an office. But on the day that we moved in, we were shocked to find out how filthy our new apartment was. The previous tenants were peasants who had geese, ducks, and pigs living in the apartment with them. The floor was thick with dirt. We hired two women to help us clean the apartment, and after two days of scraping, we were pleased to discover there were beautiful parquet wood floors underneath all of that grime.

George and I were very happy in our new home and began to feel settled in our new life. He bought an x-ray machine and medical equipment for his new office and I was spending time with Eva, his late brother's daughter, who had been living with us off and on since 1946, because her mother could not handle the squabbling amongst her children.

Then one day in 1948, the chief of the pediatrics department made a comment to George: "I hate those lousy Germans." Surprised by the comment, George replied, "But you were always a fascist. I thought you liked the Germans."

"Yes, but we paid them three thousand crowns per Jew to kill them and too many of them came back. Next time, we will do it ourselves. Next time, none of them will come back."

George knew it was time to leave Czechoslovakia. The following Friday, I went to work on getting George a passport, which required me to travel to Bratislava and Prague. My own passport had been reissued the year before. At the time, I had to go to the police station in Presov to pick up official papers allowing me to leave the country. I was so frightened at the possibility of being retained by the communist police, I made George accompany me to the station. I did not want to be separated from him again. At the station, the chief of police took one look at my American passport and said, "You are lucky. I wish it were mine."

To begin the process of getting George's passport,

I left Presov for Kosice and took the train to Bratislava. When I arrived at the Ministry of Internal Affairs in Bratislava, one of the two clerks in charge of the passports asked me, "Is Dr. Oravec a lawyer or a medical doctor?" I told her he was a medical doctor.

"Then we cannot sign the application because there is a shortage of doctors. He cannot leave," she declared. I had already paid fifty thousand crowns for the passport. I glanced at the other clerk, who had recognized me from my days as a lawyer, when she was a court recorder in the small town of Medzilaborce. She looked at me and then asked her colleague: "Listen, do you have this law in black and white? Her colleague said that she did not, but had overheard her boss talking to Prague on the telephone. Her colleague replied, "That means you were eavesdropping on your superior." In Communist Czechoslovakia, eavesdropping was against the law. Then she said to her colleague: "If you sign the application, we won't tell your boss that you were listening in on his conversation." With that, the clerk signed the application.

I telephoned George immediately and told him that he had to get on the next train to Prague because there was trouble with his passport. The next morning, George and I met at the train station in Prague. From there, we went directly to the Ministry of Internal Affairs. Before George's passport could be released to him, he had to get it signed at the Ministry of Social Services. As we were walking out the Ministry of Internal Affairs building around nine in the morning, suddenly all of the lights around us went out. There was a power outage in the city. The streetcars were not running and we could not find an available taxi. I went up to a police officer and asked for directions to the Ministry of Social Services. He told me it was clear across town and that he thought we would not be able to make it there on time. On Saturdays, the Ministry was only open until one o'clock in the afternoon. Just then, a small man with an attaché case who was leaving the ministry building approached us. He looked at George and asked him, "Are you George Oravec?" George told him yes, and the man replied, "I have your passport here." He was taking the passport to the Ministry of Social Services and suggested that we walk there together. George gave him one hundred crowns. On the way there, we hailed a taxi and the three of us shared a ride to the Ministry, where George's passport was finally issued.

The next day, George and I were on the train to Paris. While we had been able to recover the valuables that Jolan's friend had hidden for us during the war, the government had imposed severe restrictions on what George and I could take out of the country. On the day of our trip, I wore every piece of jewelry that I owned, hoping that customs officials would presume by my gaudy display that I was wearing only costume jewelry and, as such, would not question the value of it or confiscate it. I looked like a Christmas tree.

George and I stayed in Paris for three weeks before sailing on the Queen Elizabeth to New York. At the time Sanyi was the chief of the Jewish Joint Distribution Committee in Paris and was living there with his wife Natalie, where their two daughters would later be born. While in Paris, Lori wrote to tell us that two days after we left Czechoslovakia, the government was looking for George because they wanted to revoke his passport.

As soon as we boarded the ship to America, George spent half of the ten dollars we had with us to buy me a deck chair. But, I never had a chance to sit in the chair because I spent most of the five-and-a-half days on board ship vomiting over the edge of the deck. By the time we arrived in New York, I was weak from dehydration.

CHAPTER TEN

New York City

George and I arrived in New York City in March of 1949. Waiting for us at the dock were Ilonka, Zoli, Icu, and Rozsi. Immediately after the war, Icu worked with the UNRRA helping people in Yugoslavia. By the time of our arrival, Ari and Stephanie were living in Budapest. Ari had accepted a position as vice president of the Jewish Joint Distribution Committee in Prague and Budapest and Icu had taken over Ari's role at The Jewish Home for the Aged in Manhattan. While in Budapest, Stephanie gave birth to Alan, their only child. They would eventually move back to America in 1951.

Ilonka, Zoli, and Rozsi had also spent time in the concentration camps. Zoli had developed a severe Vitamin A deficiency while in camp that left him temporarily blind. After months of recuperation, his vision was restored; however, four years after liberation, it was apparent that his poor health lingered on.

At the dock, Icu offered me some coffee, but at that point, I could not even bear to smell food. When Ilonka mentioned that we would be taking the subway to her home. I replied, "No! Do not put me on anything that moves!" and suggested that we walk home instead. They all laughed at me and then I was told that if I started walking now, in twenty-four hours, I still would not make it to Ilonka's apartment in the Bronx. I relented and we took the subway.

When we arrived at my sister's apartment, I pointed to a door in the hallway and asked what it was. I was told it was a closet. "Good to know," I thought to myself. Then I went into their bedroom. There, I saw two more doors and asked what they were. Again, I was told they were closets. I walked down the hall and noticed a bathroom. I shook my head and thought, "Crazy Americans. Four toilets for two people." In Europe, toilets were known as water closets. Clothes closets were not built into our homes; instead, we hung our clothes in wardrobes.

The day after our arrival in New York, George suggested that we take the subway into the Slovak neighborhood so he could buy me a Slovak-English dictionary. While George had a cursory knowledge of English, I had none. When we were walking near the bookstore, I mentioned to George that I needed to use the rest room. He suggested that I use one of the facilities in the subway. When I said, "But I do not know where the subway is," he replied, "Ask someone." Then he taught me how to say, "Where is the nearest subway?" in English and told me that he would meet up with me later at the subway.

As I walked down 75th Street, I repeated to myself in English, "Where is the nearest subway?" When I posed the question to the next passerby, he responded with, "Which one, 72nd or 79th?" I did not know there were so many entrances to the subway. Then I noticed a group of people heading down a flight of stairs and followed them down to the subway. After I had used the rest room, I waited for more than an hour for George to return. Shortly thereafter, I noticed there were trains going to the Bronx, so I got on one. On the train I asked a German-speaking woman if the train was going near Topping Avenue. She said that Topping Avenue was in the West Bronx and that I was on a train to the East Bronx. I would have to take a cross-town bus to get home. After I had paid for the subway fare, I had no more money, but the bus driver gave me a token for the trip home. Later, when George arrived back at my Ilonka's, he was white as a sheet. He told Zoli that he was certain that he had lost me.

George and I began to rent a room on the sixth floor of a rooming house on 103rd Street. For two dollars a day, we had a small room to ourselves and shared a kitchen and bathroom with six other families living on the floor. Most of the families were from

Puerto Rico. I found living there very difficult. If I put something in the refrigerator, it was gone in an instant. I never saw the sky from our room because a tall building with electric lights on it obscured the view, and our room was sweltering hot in the summer. To cool off at night, George and I walked to the shores of the Hudson River, where outdoor concerts were held. We sat by the water listened to the music until midnight, then walked back to our apartment.

After a few weeks living in America, I was eager to start work. When Ilonka first arrived, she worked in a slipcover factory. I got a job sewing in the same factory. Before I started the job, I thought I knew how to sew, but the industrial machines were too strong and fast for me to operate well. When my boss saw that I was having difficulty, I was re-assigned to folding the covers. The job paid sixty cents an hour.

When George and I arrived in New York, Ilonka was working as a housekeeper at The Jewish Home for the Aged. Later, she and Zoli moved to Memphis, Tennessee, after she accepted a better housekeeping job there. I got a job in the laundry room in the basement of the Jewish home folding old people's underwear and shirts.

The hot summer weather, coupled with the heat and steam from the industrial washers and dryers, made the basement stifling hot. There was no relief outside—even the asphalt on the street was melting in the hot sun. But my new job paid me one hundred twenty dollars a month.

I started to study English as a child might learn the language. I read every sign I saw and listened to every word said by others. But the new language continued to confound me. One day, I passed a sign that read, "Store for Rent." *Store* is the Hungarian word for draperies. I took pity on this poor person—one so poor that he was trying to rent his drapes. I began to read *The New York Mirror*, a newspaper that was filled with photos, making it easier to figure out what the stories were about. My knowledge of Latin and French made English a little easier to comprehend. Within six months of my arrival, I was speaking English rather well.

Before my supervisor went on vacation, she told me to write a journal in English of everything I did during the day. This also helped me learn the language. Six months after I started working for her, I became her assistant. I had a new monthly salary of one hundred eighty-five dollars and had nearly one hundred people working under me.

George had begun to study English quite seriously as soon as we had arrived because he had to pass a language exam before he could take his New York State medical examination. He learned the language in three months. English was now the tenth language that George had mastered. He was already fluent in Slovak, Czech, Hungarian, Russian, German, French, Greek, Latin, and Hebrew.

In June 1949, two months after we arrived, George took the New York State medical license exam. Six weeks later he was notified that he had passed. The speed with which George was able to learn English and pass his state license exam was unprecedented: No immigrant had ever taken and passed the New York State medical exam in such a short time.

In June, before he even knew if he had passed the license exam, George was recommended for an internship at the Metropolitan City Hospital, where he worked a shift of thirty-six hours on and twelve hours off and earned fifty dollars a month.

After a year of working at the hospital, George opened his own practice on 185th Street and the Grand Concourse in the Bronx. But, because there were so many doctors in the area, after six months, George saw no patients. One day, he paid five dollars to take a taxi to his new patient in the East Bronx. When George returned home, he told me that the patient was too poor to pay him, so the house call cost him ten dollars. About that time, George decided that it was time to "go somewhere where they need me." He read in a medical journal that there were doctor positions available in Ohio. He wanted to set up a practice in Wellsville, Ohio, but even with the help of Wellsville's mayor, we had a difficult time finding a place in town that was available to rent. While we were waiting for a vacancy, George saw an ad for a doctor's position in a hospital in Cambridge, Ohio. He applied and was accepted and signed a three-month employment contract with the hospital.

CHAPTER ELEVEN

Wellsville

By the time George's contract with the hospital in Cambridge had ended, the mayor of Wellsville had found an apartment for us to live in. Shortly thereafter we moved to Wellsville, a small town about sixty miles from Cambridge, where George set up his medical practice.

In August of 1951, I became pregnant again. I stayed off of my feet during that time, but three months later, I miscarried. A few days after my miscarriage, I still felt pregnant. George thought that my nausea was psychosomatic. But days later, when the feeling did not subside, George examined me and said, "Esther, I think you have a tumor. We will have to go to the university hospital in Pittsburgh to have you checked out." I asked him, "Can we wait four weeks?" and he said yes. Then, a week or two later, I felt a slight kick in my womb. George examined me again and confirmed what I had felt all along. Indeed, I was carrying another baby.

Hoping it would help me carry my baby to full term, I stayed off of my feet for the remainder of my pregnancy. We rented a stretcher and every morning, before they went to work, George and a neighbor lifted me onto the stretcher and carried me from my bedroom to the sofa in our living room. George turned on the television set for me and I lay there all day, a captive audience to whatever program happened to be on. Back then, there were no remote controls for changing channels, so every morning, I watched the children's show, "Captain Kangaroo."

On Easter Sunday, April 13, 1952, our daughter Judy was born. Right after she was born, I discovered that I was unable to sit up. The pain in my back from being forced to lie down for six months was unbearable. It hurt so much to sit up that I could not even feed my baby. I told George that I could not take care of our baby and that we would have to return to the hospital. For eight days, the hospital nurses fed Judy and I walked to retrain and strengthen my back muscles.

In 1954, when Judy was two years old, we moved to a large house in Wellsville in which George set up his practice. Around this time, I became pregnant again, but lost the baby late in my pregnancy. When I came home from the hospital after the loss of my baby, Judy was waiting for me at the top of the stairs. She looked at me and said, "Where's Jimmy?"

Judy liked to call the baby in my womb, "Jimmy."

When I responded that Jimmy was now in heaven, she looked sad for a moment. Then her face brightened and she said, "Now you can carry me!"—an exciting notion for her because I was not able to pick her up during my pregnancy.

Judy was a very bright and curious child. George took an active interest in educating her. Just before the Christmas holiday, when Judy was two-and-a-half years old, George took her for a walk to the five-and-dime. At the store they saw a display of artificial and live Christmas trees. George pointed to one of the fake trees and said to Judy, "That is an artificial tree." Then he pointed to a live tree and said, "This is a real tree." A little later, when we were visiting our friend who was a priest, George said to Judy, "I am your father and Father John is a father. So what kind of father is Father John?" Judy shouted, "An artificial one!"

George talked to Judy about everything and encouraged her analytical mind. When she was five, he taught her about the stages of life. He placed fertile chicken eggs in his incubator, then Judy and he opened a few of them at different stages in their development. Later, Judy took the incubator to school to let her classmates watch several of the eggs hatch. George also taught her how to churn butter. When Judy was twelve, he introduced her to calculus and at age thirteen, she enrolled in a four-week college math course at Case Western University. When George asked her professor how well Judy was doing in the class, the professor replied, "She is the best in the class; but, she is immature for an eighteen-year old." That is when George informed him that Judy was only thirteen years old.

At age sixteen, Judy graduated from high school; at twenty, she graduated from Oberlin College. After college, she enrolled at the University of Chicago Medical School. Upon graduation, she completed her internship and residency at Columbia University Presbyterian Hospital in New York and became a board-certified internist. Later, she was accepted at Stanford Hospital, where she earned a subspecialty in gastroenterology.

Judy Kemeny at age 3.

The Kemeny residences in Wellsville, Ohio.

CHAPTER TWELVE

Chicago

While Judy was still in medical school, George took a postgraduate course at The Chicago Medical School. One day the professor who was teaching the course came up to him and said, "You know more than I do!" and asked George if he would like to teach at the school. George accepted the offer, and in 1973, we moved to Chicago and George began his decade-long teaching career. He was an assistant professor at The Chicago Medical School until the school moved to North Chicago. In 1976, he began teaching at the University of Illinois, where he was associate director of its Family Practice Center until his retirement.

When George retired in 1983, he began to write a book on the influence of Semitic languages on Slavic and other European languages. George spent sixteen hours a day on his book. After working on it for two years, he told me, "two more years and it will be done."

Then, one day near the end of 1985, George went out for a walk. When he returned, his head and face were dripping with blood. He said, "I think somebody mugged me." We checked his pockets.

George had not been robbed. We realized that he must have lost consciousness and fallen onto the pavement. Two weeks later, George complained of a severe headache and we rushed him to the hospital. Tests revealed that George had a brain aneurysm. The next morning, George was scheduled for surgery. Just before he went into surgery, George assured me that everything would be fine. He told me that he was not worried, so I shouldn't be either. Then we kissed. But during the operation, George's heart stopped. He fell into a coma for ten days and required an artificial respirator to breathe. One day while he was still in a coma, I walked into his room and saw that his eyes had turned filmy white from cataracts. His doctors then gave me the grave news. If George were to come out of the coma, he would not have all of his faculties. I told the doctors that it was time to remove the respirator. After I made my decision, a doctor who had noticed how haggard I had become, suggested that I go to the cafeteria to eat some soup. When I returned to George's room, I approached his bedside and touched him. He was now cold.

After he was gone, a nurse who had cared for him on the night before his surgery told me that George was very distraught that night. He had cried for hours on end and did not sleep. The last words she remembers him sobbing were, "Tell my wife that I love her very much."

Esther and George Kemeny in 1985.

EPILOGUE

After George's death in 1986, I moved to California to be closer to Judy, who, at the time was a staff internist and gastroenterologist at Kaiser Permanente Hospital in Redwood City, California. Before I left for California, I gave away most of my furniture. I did not want to bring anything with me that would remind me of the fact that George was no longer with me. I moved from Chicago to San Mateo, California, a city about fifteen miles south of San Francisco, where I lived happily for fifteen years.

In 2001, I moved into Rhoda Goldman Plaza, an assisted living facility in San Francisco, California, where I still live today.

I enjoy my home and my life here and feel fortunate to be so close to the ones I love. Today, my daughter, her husband, Paul, and my two precious grandchildren are an important part of my everyday life.

I am grateful to have known so much love in my life.

ACKNOWLEDGMENTS

I would like to thank my late husband, the beloved George Kemeny, whom I miss so much. I would also like to thank my daughter, Judy Kemeny, and her husband, Paul Feigenbaum, for their love and kindness, and for bringing Sam and Susan into our lives. Eternal love and gratitude is extended to my sister, Ilonka, and to my brothers, Icu, Ari, and Sanyi. Throughout my young life they watched over me, kept me in clothing, and supported me in so many ways. Without the love and support of my family, I could not prosper.

I would also like to thank Barry Gurdin and Mary Beth Williams, for their friendship and assistance with my original manuscript, and Heather Haller, for all of her work on this book.

Finally, I would like to thank interviewer Sue Siegel of the Bay Area Oral History Holocaust Project, to whom I first told my story in 1990, and Ruth Durling of Steven Spielberg's Shoah Foundation, who interviewed me in 1999.

Standing aloof in giant ignorance,
Of thee I hear and of the Cyclades,
As one who sits ashore and longs perchance
To visit dolphin-coral in deep seas.
So thou wast blind;—but then the veil was rent,
For Jove uncurtain'd Heaven to let thee live,
And Neptune made for thee a spumy tent,
And Pan made sing for thee his forest-hive;
Aye, on the shores of darkness there is light,
And precipices show untrodden green,
There is a budding morrow in midnight,
There is a triple sight in blindness keen;
Such seeing hadst thou, as it once befel
To Dian, Queen of Earth, and Heaven, and Hell.

"To Homer" - John Keats, 1848